HAMLET
Sports Special

Angling

HAMLET
Sports Special

Angling

Hamlyn
London · New York · Sydney · Toronto

The photographs on the cover and preliminary pages are:
Front cover A peaceful scene. Fishing for trout in a quiet stream
Back cover Salmon fishing at Watersmeet on the River Lyn, North Devon
Title spread Waiting for a bite at Weybred Pits on the Norfolk/Suffolk border, noted for its bream
Introduction page Boys fishing in a stream – where most angling enthusiasms start

This book was commissioned by 'Hamlet' Cigars

'Hamlet' and 'Benson and Hedges' are registered trade marks in the United Kingdom of J. R. Freeman & Son Limited and Benson & Hedges Limited respectively; both companies are subsidiaries of Gallaher Limited

Acknowledgements

The pictures in this book were obtained from the following sources:

Hamlyn Group Picture Library: 8, 9 (both), 15 (lower), 18-19, 35, 43, 55, 58, 64 (lower); William J. Howes (Angling Photo Service): 26, 33 (lower), 40, 41, 42, 46, 47, 48 (both), 49, 50, 52, 56 (upper), 61 (top), 65, 68 (lower), 69 (lower), 75, 76 (lower), 79, 80-81, 83, 84 (top and centre), 85 (lower), 86 (lower), 89, 91, 92 (top), 93, 96; Mansell Collection, London: 10, 11, 12, 13, 14, 15 (top), 16 (both); Spectrum Colour Library, London: 30, 34 (lower); Tony Stone Associates, London: front cover; Barrie Welham: 31, 33 (upper); Ken Whitehead: 54, 64 (top right); Zefa/Bob Croxford: 7

The remaining photographs were supplied by Mike Millman, Plymouth.
Special artwork was drawn by Brian Robertshaw.

Published 1981 by
The Hamlyn Publishing Group Limited
London · New York · Sydney · Toronto
Astronaut House, Feltham, Middlesex, England

ISBN 0 600 34655 2

Phototypeset by Photocomp Limited, Birmingham, England
Printed in Italy

Contents

Introduction

Benny Green

In his introduction to this second Hamlet Sports Special, *Benny Green confesses that he and angling are complete strangers. However, while he cannot pass on any great words of advice or reminiscence to the avid reader, he does at least have some views on the place of fish in literature, such as* The Racing and Football Outlook . . . .

In that classic among sporting books *The Compleat Angler*, Isaac Walton speculates as to whether any mere book can ever hope to turn a man into an angler. If I am anything to go by, the thing is impossible, for I have read Walton and yet never so much as flung a pin into a puddle in the hope of coming up with anything fishy. But if any book has a chance of pulling off Walton's difficult trick, then this one is probably it. Being myself one of those townees who was 19 years old before he discovered that haddock are not born in vinegary back numbers of *The Racing and Football Outlook* armoured in brown batter with crackling crumbs in the corners of their eyes, many technical terms to be found in the following pages strike me as being obscure to the point of religious mysticism, and yet I have to say that they do somehow convey to me a vague impression of the thrill your dedicated angler experiences every time he casts off. (For years I thought that this technical expression was to do with knitting, but I see now that I was wrong.)

As to this failure of mine ever to attempt to catch anything, it probably has much to do with how I began. I appear to have got off on the wrong fin. My first exposure to the art of angling was in the pages of *Three Men in a Boat*, in which hilarious work I read of the angler who was so honest about the size of his catch that he decided to limit his lying to 25 per cent of the truth, only to go raving mad trying to work out what 25 per cent of three trout came to. From that day I proceeded on the assumption that Angling was supposed to be harmlessly funny – unless you happened to be a fish –

and was therefore rather shocked by the landlocked boorishness of Dr Johnson's ponderosity to the effect that a fishing rod was a stick with a hook on one end and a fool on the other. (That in this case the fool was Johnson himself was a subtlety which did not occur to me for some considerable time – about 5 minutes.)

Since then I have learned to take both the pro and con of angling lobbies as they come, and to expect either of them to pop up at the most unexpected times in the most incongruous contexts. The most surprising of these is perhaps George Orwell's novel *Coming Up for Air*, in which a writer not generally noted for his celebration of the minor pleasures of life waxes ecstatic about the delights of angling. Not content with having his hero say, apropos life's pleasures, "Fishing certainly came first, but reading came a good second", Orwell actually goes on to make pro-angling remarks so hysterical as to be utterly without any meaning at all, for example, "Fishing is the opposite of war". (I have it on good authority from literary friends that Orwell eventually gave up writing about fish and won fame in other areas.)

To return to Isaac Walton, he did tend to make things difficult for the beginner by refusing to clean up his vocabulary. A versifier called Warham St Leger pinpointed Walton's annoying habit of referring to 'the Chavender or Chub' by observing:

> How good the honest gravender!
> How snug the rustic pavender!
> From sheets as sweet as lavender,
>   As lavender, or lub,
> I jump into my tavender,
>   My tavender, or tub

a rhyming device so diabolical that it quite distracts me from my original intention, which was to have ended this prefatory note by slyly observing the truth of the rustic saw, Spare the Rod, Spoil the Fish. Some other time, perhaps.

A Review of Angling History

Alan Wrangles

Probably the most fascinating aspect of angling is its almost universal appeal. People of all ages, classes, and from most parts of the world seem to have enjoyed fishing with rod, line and hook from the earliest of times.

Studying the various historical records makes the reader very aware of the incredible similarity between methods used, say, 500 years or more before the birth of Christ, and those employed by present day anglers.

Chinese literature written about 500 BC refers to the fishermen of the day using silk line, sharpened iron hooks and thorn sticks for their rods, and what is even more amazing, split grain as bait.

William Radcliffe, in his book *Fishing from the Earliest Times*, noted a sentence in Lieh Tzŭ which ran: "By making a line of cocoon silk, a hook of a sharp needle, a rod of a branch of bramble or dwarf bamboo, and using a grain of cooked rice as bait, one can catch a whole cartload of fish."

Obviously in those days, as indeed in present times, many would have fished out of necessity and not purely for pleasure; but there can be no doubting that since men first learned to catch fish on 'rod and line' some have always fished just for the fun of it.

Plutarch, a Greek writer who lived about AD 100, in mentioning angling, offered the advice that hairs from a white horse should be used next to the hook. He also recommended that as few knots as possible be tied in the line, advice which would not be out of place today.

It is, of course, highly probable that many tribes or races used rods and lines to catch fish, long before they developed the means to record their actions. Also, the primitive equipment used in those far off times would have long since decayed, for it is only in the dry warm atmosphere of some deserts that such artefacts would have survived.

It is hardly likely that angling began just as man discovered how to mark his progress in picture and word.

Angling as a recreation could well have been more a part of the leisurely warmer climes rather than the colder, harder north lands where activities like catching fish were increasingly likely to be aimed at raising or collecting food.

Possibly only young Vikings sat and fished from the rocky edges of their native fjords – but fish they did, and with line and hook. For not only was a hook discovered in a grave dating from about AD 150, but Stone Age bone hooks have been found in Norway, providing proof that for 5,000 years or more, baited hooks have been used to catch fish in European waters.

Caxton, the first English printer, set up a press at Westminster around 1477. As this new process spread so the first books on the art of angling appeared and among the earliest was *The Treetyse of Fysshynge wyth an*

An early angler is this nude Greek catching fish around 500 BC

Angle, supposedly compiled by Dame Juliana Berners.

This was the fourth part of the 1496 second edition of *The Book of St Albans*, a volume mainly devoted to hunting, hawking and armorial ensigns worn by knights.

If Dame Juliana Berners was the compiler of this book, and there are those who have expressed some doubt, she might be called the mother of British angling.

However, there is no doubting that Isaak Walton is the father, for no other name is more closely associated with angling than his.

Born in August 1593, Walton enjoyed a long life which spanned four reigns and the Cromwellian Commonwealth, and when he died in 1683, he was buried in Winchester Cathedral.

The first edition of his world famous book *The Compleat Angler* was published in 1653. In such times, fishing for sport was mainly a recreation for those who possessed both the time and money to indulge themselves. Also, it would have been difficult for the majority to approach a river or lake without trespassing. In those days the results of being caught in such circumstances could be extremely unpleasant. Indeed fishing itself could not always have been particularly pleasurable, especially when the antics performed whilst taking a large fish are considered.

In the days when your line was fixed to the rod tip, it was common practice when a large fish was hooked, to throw the rod into the water and let the fish tire itself out towing the rod. You then recovered the rod from the water. Just imagine splashing through a stream in February or March chasing a lively salmon for an hour or so. In those days, in those ways, you really earned your fish.

In fact it was not until 1650 or so that the use of a running line was first mentioned by the writer T. Barker, but no doubt it was a long time before the practice was widely adopted.

Much before this, in 1175, Richard the Lionheart was responsible for the first law which actually set out to protect fish and fishing. He laid down that a channel in the mid-stream of a river must be kept free of obstruction. The width of such a channel should be such that a well fed three-year-old pig could go down sideways on to the flow and not touch either side. The same law also prohibited fishing from sunset on

Above *An illustration of an angler from* The Treetyse of Fysshynge wyth an Angle *published in 1496*

Left *Still the most famous of fishing books: the title page of* The Compleat Angler *by Isaak Walton, published in 1653*

Saturdays until the Monday sunrise.

Much has changed since those days, but curiously very little fishery legislation was enacted until the Salmon Fishery Act, 1861; although Magna Carta did give the public a right to fish, free of charge, in the tidal section of rivers, and also from the sea shore. However, even that is not as straightforward as it sounds, because although you may have the right to fish at a certain point on the river, complications arise if the landowner restricts access: but fishery law is a massive subject in its own right.

As time progressed, what has become an incredibly complex industry began to develop to supply the angler with an increasingly wide range of goods and services. Probably hook making was the basis of the industry, and in Britain the centre of this trade in the early 1600s was London. It was here that the needle makers, and the subsidiary art of hook making, flourished until 1666. Then the Plague and the subsequent Great Fire of London forced the survivors of these cottage industries out into the countryside.

Historians tell us that during the first couple of decades of the 1700s, a hook and needle industry was fast becoming established in Redditch, a Midlands town which was eventually to become widely known for its angling products. Henry Milward had a needle-making business there in 1730 and within a hundred years hook makers in Redditch had become suppliers to the world. Samuel Allcock started here, and over the years this firm was moulded and built into what many have described as 'the largest tackle business in the world.' Sadly, it is no more.

But what of the angler himself? The average working man probably had some inclination, but very little spare time, to indulge in fishing for fishing's sake. In those days when work was the master of most waking hours, survival was the name of the game, and so to the average workman, angling would more than likely have meant no more than the capture of food.

However, with the industrial revolution forcing more and more change at an ever increasing pace, there grew the beginnings of the modern angling scene.

Around 1830 the item which was to become universally known as the

An angler catches a cat at Hampton in this plate from an early nineteenth-century book

PILGRIMS FISHING at HAMPTON

ANGLERS OF 1811.

A humourous painting of anglers having more fun than luck in 1811

Nottingham reel made its appearance, and silk line with silk worm gut casts were well known by coarse anglers who fished from about 1850 onwards.

It was during this period that freshwater competitive angling began to grow. 'Match fishing', as it is now called, has become a science – indeed many items of equipment, styles of angling and rod improvements are directly attributable to those who have come to specialise in this highly competitive sport.

Match fishing has its roots very firmly planted in the Midlands and North, and I feel that no survey of this sort, however brief, would be complete without reference to the description of an early match by J. W. Martin in his splendid book *Coarse Fish Angling*, published in 1908.

He writes about a match he saw some 35 years previously: "This particular match had only about 50 contestants, but they must have selected themselves from the very scum of the Sheffield dregs; they were, I was informed, a party of the very lowest of the low grinders, men whose every word was an oath; men who exchanged compliments so painful and free that I should have thought would have blistered the tongues that uttered them.

"These men consumed more beer and tobacco than was good for them, and in short conducted themselves in such a manner that any respectable angler who was looking on felt ashamed of himself and the company he found himself in."

He continued his graphic description with remarks relating to the conduct of the anglers as they drew numbers from a hat, numbers which would settle where each would fish.

"I remember No. 10 by some means hit No. 11 on the head with his long, two jointed landing handle, and No. 11 retaliated with a few choice and extra painful remarks, and then the next man, No. 12, joined in, and courteously reminded No. 11 that he would punch his head off if he so much as threw his bait one inch into his swim. No. 13 was amusing himself in the interim of getting ready by cursing the officials and all the general match arrangements, the most curious part of this being that he wore a director's rosette, and had helped to make those arrangements himself. Every now and again, one of the competitors would yell at the top of his voice to another fifty yards away to enquire in language more forcible than polite if he had 'copped owt yet' and that one would reply in still more forcible terms, 'Ave I ——.' We need not fill this up."

Times change, but, one is tempted to ask, does human nature?

At that time game fishing, the pursuit of salmon and trout, was the preserve of the well to do. Sea angling? Well, original hand-lines accomplished as much as was needed and few rods were in general use.

which occurred just after the Second World War.

It was back in 1905 that Holden Illingworth developed the first fixed spool reel, and two years later produced the second version which was complete with alternative left or right hand wind, slipping clutch – in fact just about everything we know today except for the automatic line pick up.

However, this reel never took hold of the

An engraving from a painting by P. Nasmyth called 'The Angler's Nook', showing the pleasures of fishing in solitude around 1820

Opposite Fashionable ladies joining in the catching of bass in 1884

However the 1920s and 1930s saw a steady, if undramatic rise in the popularity of this type of sport.

Over the years tackle changed. Whole cane rods were fitted with tip sections made of greenheart, and various other imported and home grown woods, and eventually built cane rods were developed in both America and Great Britain at about the same time, around 1860.

Gradually the new type of rod, built cane, became widely adopted, and it remained so until the next big change

anglers' imagination – principally because the line available in those days just did not suit Illingworth's invention.

Yes, versions of Illingworth's original were made, but it was not until after the Second World War, when nylon monofilament line became universally available, that the full potential of the reel was recognised.

It happened at a time when all the conditions were right for an explosion in leisure activities. Money was available, and was rapidly becoming more so; it was

1. Drawing Numbers for Fishing Stations.
2. Weighing a Catch.
3. Suspense.

GENERAL VIEW OF THE WATER.

A   FISHING   COMPETITION   IN   LINCOLNSHIRE.

Above *Salmon fishing at Bettws y Coed near Snowdon in Wales around 1875*

Left *An angler after a second perch from* The Complete Angler, *published in London 1836*

Opposite *A page from a magazine showing a fishing competition taking place in Lincolnshire in 1890*

A proud lady photographed with a fine salmon towards the end of the nineteenth century

Trout fishing is no longer the jealously guarded privilege of the few who enjoyed access to a relatively small number of waters.

Today in the South West, in fact just Devon and Cornwall, there are eight stocked trout fisheries (reservoirs) producing some 80 thousand fish each year for the thousands of anglers who fish there. Add to this number a further seven natural fisheries, and four more mixed trout and coarse fish reservoirs, and one begins to appreciate just how much water is available on a national basis.

Today, angling is calculated to be the major participant sport. Annually, tens of thousands of pounds are offered by a variety of firms and organisations as prize money in coarse fishing competitions.

Tackle has entered the realms of high technology with carbonfibre and space age metals being used to produce seemingly near indestructible equipment.

Sea anglers hop onto transoceanic jets to reach areas where they can hunt for monsters they once read about in tales by Hemingway.

However, although the outward signs and trappings of this fascinating sport have changed dramatically, in essence angling is much as it ever was, simply the art of catching a fish on a baited hook . . .

easier to travel, and leisure time was increasing as the working week grew shorter.

Glassfibre, another war time development, became the main rod-building material, and within a few years tackle shops were packed with angling equipment from all over the world.

Suddenly, trout fishing became a sport for everyone. As each new reservoir was built, so it was stocked with rainbow and brown trout, and therefore angling as a whole gained even more impetus.

An enthusiastic sportsman spurning the footbridge and getting into the water to hook a salmon in Lough Corrib near Galway in Connemara about 1900

The Ecology of Angling Waters

Brian Robertshaw

Innumerable bodies of fresh water, occupying areas of many shapes, sizes and depths, dapple the face of the British Isles. They are of diverse origins: for example, during the Ice Age, vast glaciers moved southwards from the Arctic. These masses gouged great hollows from the earth's crust and pushed before them huge walls of boulders. When the ice cap melted and receded, the hollows filled with water. Rainwater, gathering and seeking a path to lower levels and on to the sea, was channelled and forced to follow a route dictated by topographical features, and so various streams and rivers were born.

In later years some of these rivers were dammed to hold back the great quantities of water required by increasing domestic and industrial expansion. In recent years, whole valleys have been walled and flooded to provide more and more water.

Expanding industry, looking for an easy and cheap means of transport for raw materials and finished products, created a spider's web of canals over Britain. This form of transport has declined, but many of the now disused canals provide leisure facilities for a large number of people who, for example, wish to go boating or fishing.

These variations and combinations of the fresh-water environment offer to those animals who live in fresh water many contrasting lifestyles. Their lives are affected by availability of food, cover, oxygen and, in order to ensure the continuance of the species, a suitable breeding environment.

It is impossible to organise and arrange nature into strict categories and zones; indeed, those described here may, and frequently do, overlap. Such variations must always be taken into consideration.

Typical 'trout zone' landscape, high in the mountains or hills, with swift currents falling into occasional deep pools

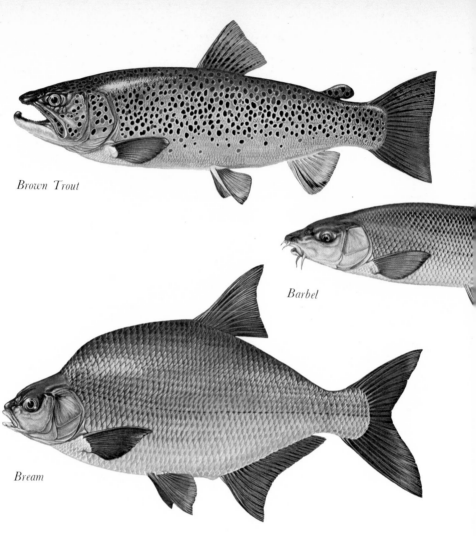

Fish which typify the five zones of a river: the trout zone, the grayling zone, the barbel zone, the bream zone and the brackish zone, from which the flounder has been chosen as an example

Brown Trout

Barbel

Bream

A general study of the lifestyles and habitats of fresh-water fishes will greatly enhance the angler's chances of success in the pursuit of his chosen sport.

Theoretically, a river, from source to estuary, may be divided into five zones. Not every river will have all these zones, but each has one or more, and each zone is conveniently named after the fish species dominant in it.

Where a river originates in mountainous or hilly country, typified in Britain by Northern England, Scotland and Wales, the first stretch of water is called the 'trout zone'.

Short swift rushing torrents, rapids and waterfalls interspersed by dark, deep pools of quieter water are characteristic of this zone. The wild gyrations of these tumbling waters aid the absorption of large quantities of oxygen, and consequently the levels of this element, which is essential to life, are extremely high. However, the water's temperature seldom exceeds 10°C (50°F) even in high summer.

In addition to trout, which in this region are usually small, wiry and with non-migratory habits, one frequently finds bullhead (millers thumb), the nocturnal loach, and in the lower limits of the zone, minnow. The invertebrates, the larvae of caddis (sedge) flies, mayflies and midges, generally live amongst the stones and pebbles which form the floor of the water course. These animals have various attributes such as claws, suction pads, and frequently a streamlined shape to enable them to move about and yet not be swept away by the strong flow. Others will build tubes or tunnels in which to live on or among the stones. Plant life is very sparse, and is generally confined to liverworts,

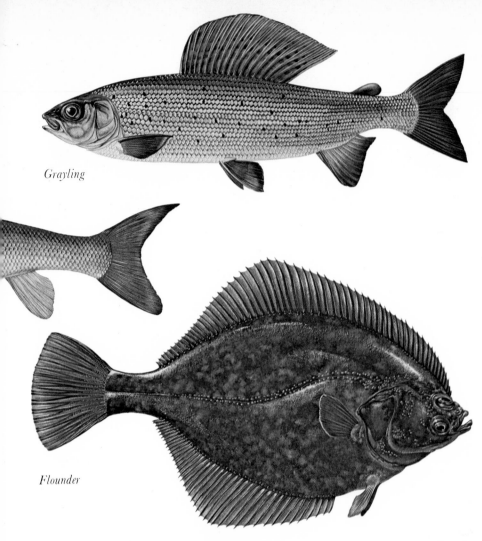

Grayling

Flounder

As the river moves to the sea, mudbanks will be formed as the current carves a channel around the outside of bends, or as the tide washed in and out at the estuary

mosses and lichens. These are able to survive submersion when melting snow or heavy rain raises the water level. Rough upland grasses and reeds may overhang the banks, but pebbles on the stream floor provide no hold for rooted plants.

Some rivers originate from springs in lowland areas; possibly the water rises up through deep chalk deposits formed in the Cretaceous period approximately 125-75 million years ago. Such rivers, typified by the Test and Itchin of Hampshire, may descend less steeply than those originating in mountains and hills but, nevertheless, the first sector should still be regarded as the 'trout zone'.

water is now much greater. Willow and alder overhang long stretches of the river bank, providing shade and cover, whilst on parts of the river bottom where coarse sand has been deposited, starfoot, crowfoot and willow moss will find a medium in which to root.

On straighter stretches of the river in this zone, long banks of well-washed, coarse gravel are often found. It is here that hen salmon and trout choose to cut their redds, trenches in which their eggs are laid. The redds can be spotted by the experienced eye, marked by the lighter colour of the newly turned gravel.

Grayling, after which the zone is named,

Typical 'grayling zone' water, still fast and rich in oxygen, but with a greater variety of plants and more trees to provide shade than the trout zone

The 'grayling zone' is next, and is closely linked to the trout zone. In fact it is often difficult to decide where one ends and the other begins! This section of the river is still very rich in oxygen but is a little warmer during the summer months: 15°C (59°F). The invertebrates are still predominantly those found in the trout zone, but the diet of fishes in this region is enhanced by the addition of some molluscs such as limpet, spine shell and bladder snail. Crayfish may also be found, and these are in many instances regarded as the finest possible bait for some species of fish. However, if you discover them, leave them where they are as, sad to say, they are an endangered species.

The variety of plants in and out of the

are beautiful fish with dark zig-zag markings along the flanks, and a large dorsal fin with orange, brown and yellow blotches. The title often given to this fish, 'lady of our streams' is very fitting. In addition, this zone may hold minnow, dace and gudgeon, whilst occasionally pike and chub will take up residence in a corner sheltered from the main current. From this position, they will take small fish or snatch other titbits on passage downstream.

The part of the river dominated by the salmonidae ends at the lower limit of the 'grayling zone.' Below this boundary they will be quickly replaced by the members of the carp family (Cyprinids), and it is one of that group which lends its name to the next area – the 'barbel zone.'

'Barbel zone' landscape. The river gets wider and flows more smoothly

Here, the water moves smoothly. There are long glides, some deep pools and still the occasional waterfall. The river is generally wider and begins to meander, cutting steep banks on the outer curves where the current is strongest, and depositing gravel, sand and mud on the inner curves which are swiftly populated by plants. Often the first are coltsfoot, dock, and willow herb whose roots help to bind together the sandy mud. Large areas of the bottom are laid with mud which supports a much greater variety of plant life. Watercress, curled pondweed, and fennel-leafed pondweed thrive here. Along the banks reed grass mingles with stitchwort, water speedwell and forget-me-not. This greenery in and out of the water supports an equally expanded range of insects, and where the water is soft, molluscs such as the valve snail and Jenkins spire shells will appear, and where the water is hard, one will find in addition the lake limpet, nerites, vortex and Listers river snails.

The range of fish species will also show a dramatic increase. Roach will shoal in the streamy runs between the reed beds, whilst the dandy perch, which wanders over large areas, is now found in great profusion. In quiet backwaters, there will often be a large solitary perch which has declared his territory and will defend it fiercely.

The 'bream zone'. The water meanders slowly through the valleys, with a large variety of trees, bushes, rushes and other water plants at its edges or on its banks

The fourth zone – the last which may be regarded as truly fresh water, is the 'bream zone'. Mountains or hills have now been left far behind, and the river meanders over the floor of a wide valley, and then perhaps to a broad plain. The flow is slow and the water turbid. At this stage the river is carrying large amounts of disolved minerals, which at times of flooding will be spilled over the surrounding land. These minerals form the basis for the formation of lush water meadows.

In some areas, Water Authorities have resorted to 'canalisation'. This wonderful word describes the following alterations to the natural river. Curves and bows are bypassed creating a featureless canal-like stretch of water. The river bed is dredged and the banks raised, often destroying the plants and dependent insect life in the process – without these, the fish will move elsewhere in search of food. It is true that these changes will prevent some flooding but, after rain, the water is allowed to rush straight to the sea carrying with it the essential minerals required to provide nourishment for plants, insects and fishes. However, it would seem that the adverse implications of these 'improvements' are now more fully appreciated, and more thought is given to a project before irreparable damage is done.

Numerous varieties of trees and bushes form curtains along the bank (the wise angler learns to use this cover). Thick rich mud in unpolluted rivers supports great masses of water plants: milfoil, bistort, hornwort and water buttercup weave and sway in the slow moving current. Along the banks are many marginal plants: rushes, water mint and the balsam with its pink flowers and amazing seed pods which startle the unwary when they explode, scattering their seeds over wide areas. Yellow flag, loosestrife, dock and mint collect a host of insect life and, attracted by this living larder, rudd will be one of the fish species here. Common and silver bream dip in search of the algae, midge larvae and tubiflex worms. These slab-sided fishes will often be joined by the golden-eyed tench, and in backwaters, carp are frequently encountered. Other fishes in this area include the bleak and three and ten-spined stickleback, and the main predatory fish are pike and the more recently introduced zander (pike-perch).

The river bed might hold numerous rocks and hollows. These give rise to fascinating swirls and eddies, which the angler may use to locate these spots, and consequently the fishes which use them as cover.

Occasionally, one may see species in the lower reaches of the 'bream region' which are really sea fishes. The best known of these are bass, mullet, flounder, smelt and shad. However, these are more closely associated with the last of the river regions – the 'brackish zone.'

This is an area of constant change – tidal movement causes the fresh and salt water to mix, and three levels may be defined vertically. The upper layer consists of fresh water moving seawards, the lower heavier layer is salt water from the sea, and sandwiched between is a strip of brackish water, a mixture of the upper and lower layers. This is an area where there are often large expanses of mud banks which have been built by the settlement of sediment carried down by the river. The organic matter in the mud provides food for large numbers of worms (lug and rag), crust-

The 'brackish zone', where fresh and salt water mix, and where dwell migratory creatures who can move between the two

aceans, such as the shore crab, prawn and shrimp, and large colonies of various molluscs. These creatures are well able to cope with the constant changes in the salinity levels typical of this zone.

There are other creatures which are migratory in their habits, moving from salt to fresh water and vice versa, just pausing long enough to allow adjustment to both salinity changes and diet. The former is made possible by special kidney functions which keep the salts within the body at an acceptable level.

There are two forms of migration. The anadromous, represented by salmon, sea trout and the sturgeon, which is now almost extinct in British waters, grow to maturity in the sea and return to the rivers to breed. On the other hand, the cata-dromous breed in the sea and return to fresh water to mature. Examples of these are some forms of flounder and the eel.

Although much too long and complicated to relate in full here, mention must be made of the extraordinary life cycle of the eel. These fish will survive in fresh water which is so heavily polluted that many other species would perish. The eel's eggs are laid in the South West Atlantic, in the areas of the Sargossa Sea, and after

23

A weed-covered swim likely to be found in the lower zones and on the inner curves of the river

with this weed and allowed to float freely in the vicinity of these and similar structures will often fool one of these shy fish).

In addition to the fishes mentioned at the beginning of this section, other sea fishes move into the brackish zone on the high tides. For example, in the Gravesend area of the Thames, cod, whiting, and occasionally haddock have been caught. Sometimes it is possible to catch these fish even further up the tidal section of the Thames.

Fish removed from the grids which cover cooling intakes of power stations situated on the shores of esturial zones provide evidence of the wide variety of fish found in the area. For example, buried in the sands of the estuary, with only eyes and dorsal spines exposed, one may find a venomous weaver – treat it with respect – and in some areas even stingray, often thought of as a tropical fish, may be trodden on or caught. Beware of the barbed spike on the upper surface of the tail; these fish can drive it into a bare foot or hand, and then medical attention is needed.

All rivers will have some of the features described here in their make-up. However – it must be stressed – not all will have every zone. This is a condensed description of the complexities of river life both above and below the water's surface.

Of course, not every fresh-water environment is centred upon a river or stream, termed 'moving water'. Biologists recognise a second locale: 'still water'. It is necessary to emphasise once more that the divisions which follow form a guide. They are not strict divisions; variations and combinations certainly exist.

In general, still waters consist of a number of types of lakes and ponds and the lakes may be divided into the 'primitive' and 'evolved.'

First the *primitive*: these are usually found in hills and mountains and were created by glacial activity some thousands of years ago. They are deep, cool and well oxygenated, but soft water is very poor in mineral content (oligotrophic) and the plant life is very sparse. The dominant fish species are the whitefishes and the trout which roam the open areas of the upper levels of the lake, and the perch, pike and some of the cyprinid fishes which may be found in the shallow waters around the shoreline.

There are small lakes found in some

hatching, the larvae drift for up to three years in the upper layers of the ocean, feeding on diatoms and being carried by the Gulf Stream towards Britain. Between January and April each year they arrive off the British coast after having metamorphosed into elvers. During the summer months they take on a darker pigmentation. Some choose to remain in the brackish waters amongst the muddy vegetation, others move up rivers into fresh water, either remaining in the river or moving into lakes and ponds, where they may remain for up to fifteen years feeding and growing. Sometimes the switch from river to lake is made over 'dry' land. Eventually their colour changes from yellow to silver, the eyes increase in size, the jaws shrink and the eel gradually ceases to take food. It is now ready to return to the sea and its birthplace, there to continue the cycle. It is a fascinating story which still lacks many factual details.

The plant life in the 'brackish zone' is generally confined to eel grass, fennel pondweed, sea purslane and marsh samphire, which at one time was gathered in great quantities and burnt – it produced soda which was used in the manufacturing processes of soap and glass. The plant's other name – glasswort – was derived from this fact.

Where there is a rocky foothold, channelled wrack and sea lettuce, together with other algae, may be found. The filamentous alga provides part of the diet for fish such as mullet, which are often seen grazing on its whiskery form around old pier supports and groynes (a hook draped

mountain areas which are known as corries or tarns. They have little or no plant life, and the survival of the small trout occasionally found in them depends on the depth of water being sufficient to prevent freezing down to the lake bed.

The *evolved* lake is typified by those bodies of water (which have formed in hollows caused by subsidence or even excavation) such as the Cheshire meres, and the fens and Broads of East Anglia. Generally shallower than the primitive lake, the water is hard and extremely rich in disolved minerals (eutrophic) – in some cases, so much so that it may be regarded as pollution. Around the margins is a rich belt of plant life. From the immediate shoreline, thick rush and reed beds may extend for some distance, at their outer limit mixing with aquatic plants with submerged leaves, such as pondweeds and milfoil, crowfoot and many others. In deeper waters there are mosses and algae, water moss and stonewort. Below about 8 metres the plants will not grow, light does not penetrate, and the bottom becomes a muddy desert.

The fish species associated with these lakes are almost identical to those found in the 'bream region' of the river: pike and perch, both varieties of bream, roach, rudd, minnow, tench and carp. Larger lone perch will often roam the deeper waters, together with the other dreaded predator, zander. The food supply for fish in such lakes is very rich and varied, in the main consisting of water fleas, lice, copepod, rotifers, protozoa, midge and alder larvae together with a wide variety of molluscs, worms and shrimp – a wonderful larder.

These lowland lakes are much more prone to pollution than are the high primitive lakes. The pollutants may take many forms and have various results. Intensive farming methods employ chemicals for pest control and this can have an effect on both plant and animal life.

Fertilisers washed into the water, may also create problems through over-enrichment of the water.

Untreated sewage may enter the water, but this is more commonly seen on rivers. There have been instances of chemical fouling in the vicinity of camp sites – the source being chemical toilets which are now in common use. Seepage from disposal pits is the usual cause, but some clandestine dumping has occurred. It should be said that this is not widespread, but there are thoughtless rebels and louts connected with every sport and pastime.

Incredible as it may seem, in recent years there have been problems created by bird droppings! In winter on some waters, the large numbers of migrant birds – ducks, geese and various waders – deposit an amazing weight of faeces in the water.

Water for industrial and domestic needs may be obtained from natural waters, but as has already been briefly mentioned, over the years demand has increased and no longer is it possible for natural sources to provide as much as is required; hence the reservoir. In some instances, whole valleys have been closed at their lower end by dams, and in the process of flooding, whole communities have been moved or scattered, and sometimes farming land has been lost.

If these reservoirs are constructed in high mountainous or hilly areas, they will generally take on the identity of the primitive (oligotrophic) lake, but in lowland areas they will resemble the evolved (eutrophic) waters.

In some areas the whole water is enclosed by a man-made wall, for example the Queen Mary Reservoir, at Staines, Middlesex.

Plant and insect life will develop as for either type of water, but fish may well be introduced by the Water Authority responsible for the particular area. However it is impossible to prevent the introduction of some species by other means. Birds are known to carry fish eggs on their legs and

An English deep water lake likely to contain pike, for which these anglers are spinning

plumage, and sometimes these drop off into water which is devoid of fish, but is able to support them. How can one prevent this – or even wish to?

There can be little disagreement that these waters can provide pleasure for various sports.

Mention must also be made here of the numerous ponds scattered over the countryside. Seldom very deep they are subject to several adversities. During the summer months they may be completely taken over by weed growth, and whilst this

The Grand Union Canal near Aylesbury contains good water in which a wide variety of fish life can be found

may be extremely advantageous to some aquatic insects and molluscs, or certain bird species, it does not help the angler. Secondly, during the autumn, especially if the water is surrounded by trees, thick layers of putrifying leaves lying on the bed will produce noxious gasses which can kill fish life. Also there is always a possibility of the pond freezing to its full depth in winter.

Life in these ponds varies, but often large numbers of stunted fish – perch, roach or rudd to mention a few species, may abound. However, catching these has implanted the love of angling into the hearts of many boys (and girls).

Finally, other stretches of water are formed by the canals. Are they moving or still water? The immediate impression is that they are still water, but one will find that, however imperceptibly, the water is flowing. The water supply for a canal might be drawn from an adjoining river and/or supplemented by reservoirs.

However, due to this minimal flow, these waters take on the characteristics of shallow still waters, rather than the river which they resemble.

Marginal plant life varies a great deal as does the underwater growth. It is dependent on depth and the regularity of traffic. On a busy canal, propeller-driven craft help to churn the bottom mud and so bottom weeds are given little chance of becoming well established. On the other hand, where the canal is little used, or not at all, there is a tendency for these stretches to become overgrown and completely choked with plants.

The quality of water in canals may vary a great deal. In some it can be an evil black smelling liquid more akin to soup than water, and containing little or no life. There can also be a high content of iron – every old pram and bedstead from miles around can finish its life there!

Other canals contain a good quality, sparkling water, supporting an abundance of insects and other creatures such as the larvae of the caddis, dragonfly and water beetles. Fresh-water shrimps and lice live amongst the weeds, and bivalves are common in the bottom mud.

On these lengths of canal the plant life is very rich. Yellow flag, arrowhead, bullrush and reed grow in thick fringes, and deeper in the water and totally submerged grow the hornworts and various pondweeds. Water soldier, milfoil and others may be seen above the water. In the Basingstoke canal the water fern (Azolla filicuoides) floats freely – this is one of Britain's rarest aquatic plants.

A wide variety of fish species can be found in this environment. Most of the cyprinids are represented, together with pike, perch and that fierce little creature, the stickleback.

In many parts of the country there are groups of people working voluntarily to clear and preserve canals which through neglect have become silted and overgrown.

It is interesting to note that the first canal in Britain was built by the Romans in AD

200, and it is still in use. Throughout Britain there are in excess of fifteen hundred miles of navigable canals and many of these miles are open to anglers, providing an indispensable facility.

Besides catering for the pleasure angler, the long straight miles of water and bank provide the ideal setting for fishing matches. On such water it really is the luck of the draw as the fish can be widespread, as there may be few, if any, fish holding areas.

Britain's native waters, be they river, lake or canal, are an asset which must be

animals just manage to hold onto life. For example, rocks with a small refuge beneath them can be host to a variety of creatures from ragworm to crabs seeking shelter whilst their new shell hardens. Turn the rock over, and leave it in this disturbed attitude and the refuge is gone. However, restore the rock to its original position after removing the worm or crab, and other creatures will move in and re-colonise the niche. Thus, the environment is preserved.

Digging for lug worm can leave the foreshore looking like a battlefield; apart

Preserving our water with care will enable us to continue to enjoy such peaceful pleasures as evening fishing on a tidal river

jealously guarded. It takes years for any water to reach maturity, and every effort must be made by all industries and the public to ensure they continue to provide pleasure for all.

Similar remarks can be made regarding the sea-shore, an area which is all too often subjected to totally unnecessary damage by those who seek their rest and relaxation in a marine environment. Sadly, this damage is seldom intentional. It just happens as a result of carelessness or total ignorance of the results of performing simple acts.

Bait collecting can damage, sometimes irreparably, those areas where certain

from being totally unnecessary, it is also a practice which damages the sand/mud banks in which the worms live. As the tide covers the mounds and hollows the whole area is changed. Some of the mud will be swept away and the hollows become sludgy and unsuitable areas for worms. A continuation of such practices will, over the years, change the whole environment.

Briefly, although we often refer to this planet as *our* world, it is in fact the only place in which all animals and plants can live and multiply.

Water, and its attendant life, is a delicate fabric, and we ill-treat it at our peril.

Fly Fishing for Salmon and Trout

Barrie Welham

With the exception of those rivers in the North of Scotland where 'fly only' has long been the rule, more salmon are caught by spinning and bait than with fly! This does not mean that a fly is not an effective lure – only that, on most rivers, spinning is practised more. Sometimes this is by choice, but at others because conditions on the bank make fly fishing unduly difficult or because the water is so coloured that a spinner is more likely to be seen.

That bank and water conditions can make fly fishing difficult is unquestionable. Anglers fishing such water may feel compelled to use bait, but on waters where fly fishing is practicable it is a pity that there are anglers who will take every opportunity to spin. Sometimes it is because the angler does not have confidence in the fly, but results prove that, fished correctly, the fly is effective. It is only by persisting that confidence is established, and constantly turning back to spinning will not achieve it. To hook the king of fish on a lump of ironmongery on a short spinning rod not only denies the quarry the opportunity to give of its best, but also dilutes the emotion that comes with achieving one of the greatest prizes in angling.

Why do anglers do it? The answer is not a simple one. To a lesser or a greater degree it shows a decline in sporting morals, often combined with an urge to win – irrespective of how. And of course these feelings are aggravated by the high cost of fishing and the high market value of the fish itself.

All this is regrettable from the point of view of human nature, but it is the salmon that is suffering! Stocks of Atlantic salmon have never been lower than they are now. Salmon no longer run the world's rivers in the numbers they once did. Once the decline was only gradual but in the last few years it has become dramatic. Some rivers, which afforded good sport as recently as the 1950s, now count their annual catch in tens rather than hundreds.

Many factors have contributed to the decline. Pollution, abstraction and other environmental changes are root causes. Hydro-installations, which raise water levels and deny suitable head waters to spawning fish, are another. A lethal fish disease has also taken a large toll. Even at sea the salmon has not been safe. Using modern techniques, previously unknown, vast numbers have been taken, many by fishing fleets from countries which no longer have salmon rivers of their own.

Even though anglers may not carry the greatest responsibility for the salmon's decline, it could well be that it will fall to anglers, rather than to commercial fishermen, to lead the fight for the preservation of this fine sporting fish. Anglers may have to set an example, by limiting the methods they allow themselves, and thereby reducing the number of fish taken. This might be the way to encourage the commercial interests to consider helping greater escapement, by further limiting their catch. Without some limitation, the time may not be far off when there will not be enough salmon left to catch!

Could restricting salmon fishing to "fly only" be the method to use? Certainly the reverse, putting a ban on fly fishing, would not achieve the result needed. Spinning will catch fish, even in high coloured water, when the fly is much less effective. Equally, when the water is low, a fly does not harass fish, whereas a prawn or worm can. In fact, in these otherwise impossible conditions, such baits can be very deadly.

A ban on spinning would remove a deadly weapon from the unscrupulous, for in low water it is easy to deliberately foul fish. By restricting permitted methods it would also reduce "commercialism". Gillies would gillie instead of spinning down behind the tenant rod. Anglers would not be aiming to clear their rent, and that cost-conscious approach would decline.

Maybe all this is for the future. Let us hope the need will never occur, but already the signs are that something does need to be done. In Canada, fishing for Atlantic salmon is already restricted to fly only, and in some provinces rod-caught fish cannot be sold. Perhaps those few remaining nations, which still have Atlantic salmon, have something to learn!

Salmon fly fishing can be divided into two methods: floating line, usually practised when the fahrenheit water temperature reaches the upper 40s and sinking line.

Sinking Line Technique

For sunk line work a powerful rod of not less than 13 feet is an advantage, and 16 feet or 18 feet is even better. Until the introduction of fibreglass and carbon graphite, sunk line rods were heavy and tiring

to cast. Today, rods of equal power are much lighter so length is no longer limited by personal physique.

Prior to man-made fibres, the line for sunk fly was un-greased silk. Today a dacron wetcel is standard equipment. Lines of different density are used, depending on the speed of the current, and the depth. In shallow water, the combination wet-tip or wet-belly line will get the fly down without catching the bottom, but in water more than 5 feet deep a full sinker is necessary. Water up to 10 feet needs a fast-sinking grade 2 wetcel to get the fly down. Never underestimate the buoyancy effect of streamy water, so as current speed or depth increase so must the density of your wetcel.

The reel is not over-important, but it must be well made, so as not to jam if it

A salmon landed from the rapid flow of the River Lyn

Salmon fishing from a rock bordering the River Lyon in Perthshire, Scotland

receives an accidental knock. It should have a capacity far larger than the line alone will need. The extra space should be filled with 25-lb rot-proof backing.

For the low water temperatures which occur in February, October and November, large tube flies of up to 3 inches are used. For the remainder of the sunk line season, conventional flies on size 2 to 6 double or single hooks are used. The technique is to cast across and down. The exact angle varies with the speed of the water and is something that only experience can teach. As the cast straightens the line is mended upstream so that the fly comes more slowly across the lie. The reel check is set firm and the line is tight to the reel. When a fish takes, the weight of the water on the line, coupled with the pressure from the reel check, should put the hooks well home.

Apart from the "fly only" Helmsdale,

Thurso and other similar rivers in the North, spinning is the most practised technique at the start of the season. The unusual exception is Tweed, where it is fly only from the opening day until the commercial nets come on two weeks later when spinning is also allowed. When the nets go off in mid-September, fly only again comes in and lasts until the rod season closes on 30 November (perhaps this is an indication of the co-operation which is possible between sporting and commercial interests). That the fly is effective is clear from the results achieved. The bags taken on sunk line fly compare well with results on bait. This should be enough to convince people who doubt the effectiveness of fly when the water is big and cold.

Floating or Greased Line

Before the 1930s all salmon fly fishing was with sunk line. It was then noticed that a fly fished much higher in the water was, at times, preferred to one swinging deep amongst the fish. At that time the only way to hold the fly near to the surface was to dress the line with floatant and the term "greased line" was coined. Lines are no longer greased to make them float – but the term persists.

The technique is similar to sunk line: across and down, but with warmer water fish will move quite a distance to intercept the fly, so the cast can be more square across the current. With a floating line mending is much easier, and usually made as the cast is completed, although some anglers make additional mends as the fly comes round.

Flies generally are smaller than for sunk line, but as there can be an overlap it is necessary to carry flies ranging from 4 to 10. When fish are very stale, flies as small as 12s are sometimes effective, and miniscule tubes, with only a wisp or two of hair, will take fish when larger flies are ignored.

Hook types, like fly patterns, vary from river to river and from gillie to gillie. Single hooks are popular with some but others advocate nothing but doubles. Over the years there seems to have been a swing away from singles to doubles and then to tubes. Recently, the indications are that there has been a swing back to the double hook or Esmond Drury treble.

For floating line, rods can be shorter with an easier action, and it was this chance to get away from heavy rods that was another of the early attractions of greased line fishing.

To suit the smaller rod, the reel for floating line should be lighter, but do not use anything too small. Ideally, when a fish has all the line off and is just coming on to the backing, the reel should still be three-quarters full. If the reel is too small the tapered line will take up too much of the total space. The diameter of what is then left on the spool is so small that the re-wind speed is too slow and control can be lost.

Cast strength needs to match the rod, and this is a further reason for the less powerful outfit. With a sunk line and big flies, casts having a 17-lb to 20-lb point will perform well, but casts tapering to 8 lb or 10 lb are needed for the smaller floating line patterns. As the average size of summer fish is often less than that of fish from either the spring or autumn runs, the more delicate tackle also gives better sport.

Fly Patterns

Flies are always subject to some local preferences, although anglers visiting Norway, Canada, Newfoundland and Iceland will find that many traditional UK

A fresh run salmon of 20 lb 7 oz taken on a small fly and a floating line

patterns are used in these countries. Tyings that will catch on most rivers are Jock Scott, Durham Ranger, Dusty Miller, Thunder and Lightning, Stoat Tail, Hairy Mary, Logie and Blue Charm. Carry a selection of these in a range of sizes and you never need feel lost.

In fishing, nothing is certain. "Must" and "always" are words that a wise teacher does well to avoid. Nowhere is this more true than when trying to decide when to change from a sinking to a floating line. Water temperature is the guide most frequently used, but there is no day when a switch will be unquestionably right. Even after having taken a fish on a floating line, another angler, using a sinker, can follow you through the pool and have equal success.

Such is the charm and uncertainty of salmon fly fishing!

Temperature is only a guide. Some anglers change as soon as the water reaches 46°F. Others wait for 48°F but most agree that irrespective of the precise temperature, the air must be warmer than the water for fish readily to take the small fly.

So much then for salmon. As they are so unpredictable – due to their not feeding in fresh water – success in enticing a salmon to take a fly is an exhilarating emotion unmatched in angling. The beauty of the fish, the grandeur of the rivers, and the pure power of the water makes salmon fishing something very special. Long may the salmon – so near to becoming an endangered species – continue to run.

Fly Fishing for Trout

Britain's indigenous trout is the brown, but the American rainbow has been in British waters so long that it is almost taken for granted. The only characteristic that remains as a reminder of its artificiality is that, except in just two or three rivers, rainbows do not spawn naturally in this country. Helped by man it will give its eggs for fish farm use, but will not breed when released. This means that with no natural re-generation rainbow stocking has to be repeated over and over again, but this has its advantages for it does mean that rainbows can be controlled.

By their very nature brown and rainbow trout are both lovers of running water, but, providing the water is clean and does not over-heat in summer, they will also live and thrive in still waters. Fly fishing for trout therefore divides into four main types according to these contrasting habitats: reservoirs and lochs; small stillwater fisheries; rain-fed rivers and streams; chalkstreams.

Reservoirs

As population and the needs of industry have grown, so has the demand for water. New reservoirs have been built to cope with this increased need, and it is these big new waters that have borne the brunt of the upsurge of interest in trout.

Where the new waters have overlaid rich farmland, the initial feed available to the fish has been enormous. In these conditions, fish quickly put on weight, and the quality of sport has been outstanding. Even when this first burst is over, many waters continue to give excellent fishing providing they have sound commercial management.

At one time the techniques practised on reservoirs were similar to those traditionally employed on natural lochs. Most fishing was from a boat where the technique was to drift broadside to the wind, casting a short line in front of the boat. While this stays as the basic technique on Scottish and Irish loughs and is still practised on the big reservoirs, new techniques have also been worked out.

A big reservoir can be exposed and cold. The water is also often deep and surface activity can be sparse. In such conditions, fish often lie very deep and to get the flies down, a fast sinking wetcel line is used. Because trailing behind the boat is not usually allowed, the cast is made sideways and allowed to sweep round in an arc. With two anglers, casting on opposite sides, a lane of 30-50 yards wide is fished as the boat moves downwind.

On the bank, things are different. The water may not be very deep and a floating aircel is used. By positioning himself with the wind on his side, the bank angler can let his flies be carried round by the floating line. He retrieves only slowly but is ready to lift into the fish as soon as he sees the cast draw. If the wind is blowing straight into his face, fast surface drift might prevent his flies from getting down. In these conditions he uses a sinking wetcel for, just as with sunk line salmon, he can alter the depth and speed at which the flies fish, just by switching line. The angler tries different density lines until he finds the strata in which the fish are taking.

The tackle for these reservoir techniques is different to that used for the traditional loch style. For a loch a 9–11 feet rod carrying a 6 to 7 line will be needed. On a reservoir, the rod will be of 9–10 feet but carrying lines from 7 to 10. A size 10 line is heavy, and a few years ago no-one would have used such a line for trout, but in a big wind this heavy line makes fishing possible where it might not be with anything lighter.

Long casting encourages loose line, so reels should be large in diameter to give the quickest possible retrieve, so helping to get the hooked fish quickly under control.

Small Stillwaters

Small stillwater fisheries vary from farm ponds, irrigation reservoirs and worked out

A 7 lb 9 oz brown trout from Two Lakes, the well-known stillwater fishery in Hampshire

Fly casting for trout on the River Tilse in Kent

Above *A fly fisherman displays his skill at casting*

Above right *Fully dressed traditional salmon flies. Top row: Dusty Miller 1/0, Jock Scot 4/0, Durham Ranger 1/0, Thunder and Lightning 4/0. Centre row: low water salmon patterns Blue Charm and Logie (traditional) with Blue Charm and Logie (Scottish). Bottom row: Modern hairwing patterns Stoat Tail 1/0 and Hairy Mary 1/0. Flies dressed by Michael Veale, Lanceston, Cornwall*

Right *Fishing at Manbach in the Black Forest, West Germany*

gravel pits, through to small lakes excavated solely for fishing. Amongst the first and also one of the best known of all the purpose-built small stillwater trout fisheries that now exist is Two Lakes in Hampshire. Two Lakes was started in the 1950s since which time the expertise of the owner, Alex Behrendt, as both an imaginative and successful fishery manager, has been internationally recognised. Many have learnt from him and today a host of waters, modelled on Two Lakes, exist, with the result that fly fishing on small lakes is now an important part of the trout scene.

Although fishing on small stillwaters uses techniques similar to those used on the reservoirs, small fisheries can cater for a need which the bigger waters cannot fill.

Because the average reservoir is exposed, often cold and much affected by wind, some anglers particularly the elderly, cannot always cope with the extreme conditions to which such waters are subject. The more easily sheltered small fishery fills that need. Being more sympathetic, the tackle needed is not so powerful. Rods of 8 feet to 9 feet 6 inches carrying 6 to 8 lines will cover most needs. Wading is seldom allowed and many fisheries are not large enough for boats. This causes a line problem somewhat different to that which exists on a big reservoir. In a boat, or when wading, loose line can be dropped without coming to much harm. On a bank, covered with long grass and suchlike, line does get into all kinds of snags. This is the reason

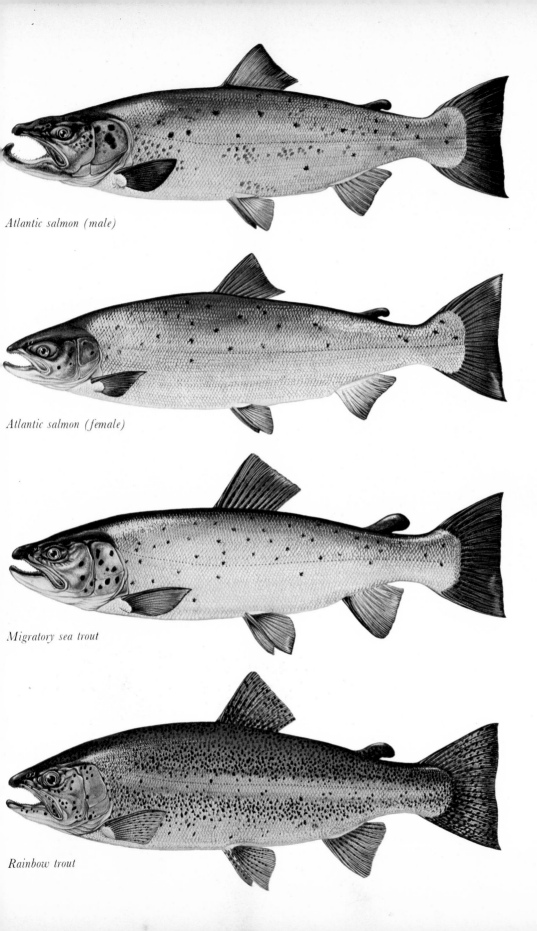

Atlantic salmon (male)

Atlantic salmon (female)

Migratory sea trout

Rainbow trout

Casting when fly fishing for trout. Top: the forward cast. Centre: the back cast as it begins to straighten. Bottom: the roller or switch cast for use when space behind is limited by trees or high banks, etc.

why so many anglers like automatic reels, which not only minimise these hazards, but also get things quickly under control when a fish is hooked and you have a lot of slack line in your other hand.

There are so many different patterns of flies for stillwaters that no list could hope to be complete. On lochs the traditional wet flies that have stood the test of time include Invicta, Butcher, Mallard and Claret, Teal and Green, Wickhams and Peter Ross. These patterns also take fish on the big reservoirs and the small stillwaters. There is also a whole range of attractor lures, and the number grows each year.

The most common insect found in stillwater is the midge larva, and patterns to represent this are legion. Again it is a question of being guided by local knowledge and your own experience. Although fishing a dry fly is very satisfying, surface food comprises only a very small part of the stillwater trout's diet. Always carry a few dry flies, for at times nothing else will do,

but most fish will be taken on something under water – be it a lure, a wet fly or a nymph.

Rivers and Streams

To leave river and stream trout to the end may seem strange, but the amount of river fishing that exists gets less all the time. Over the past 30 years abstraction has emptied many once famous streams, while others are so short of water, even in an average summer, that the weed and invertebrate ecology has changed with the result that they are no longer a suitable habitat for trout. Anglers wanting river trouting find it increasingly difficult to obtain even indifferent fishing, with the result that today there are a large number of experienced trout anglers who learnt their craft on stillwaters and have never ever had the opportunity to fish a good river.

This still deteriorating situation applies mainly to the Home Counties. In the less populated areas, where clean rivers do still exist, the fishing can be split into two general headings, one covering the rain-fed and acid rivers where fly life is sparse and fish generally small, the other the contrasting chalkstreams where insect life is plentiful enough for fish to be encouraged to look to the surface for at least some of their diet.

The Chalkstreams

The true chalkstreams are concentrated in Southern England and a small area of East Yorkshire. The two largest rivers are the Test and Itchen, which are world famous. Clear, and with a steady supply of even-temperature water, weed growth flourishes and fly life is plentiful. Dry fly upstream is the invariable rule with nymph being permitted on some beats at certain times. A downstream wet fly is never used.

One of the greatest fascinations of the chalkstreams is that you are fishing for a particular fish. Not just any fish – but a particular fish! Another is that you are trying to identify the natural fly that is hatching, and to match it with an artificial.

Having found a feeding fish it is usual to concentrate solely on that one fish until it is either caught, frightened, or goes off the feed as the hatch eventually peters out.

Their unique nature has meant that the chalkstreams have attracted far more attention from writers than the total number of anglers who fish them really warrants. Because gaining access to these rivers is far from easy, dry fly fishing has also acquired the reputation of being extremely difficult. Exacting it can be – also challenging, and because so much of what is going on is visible it is also interesting, but the technique is no more difficult than lots of other fishing, and at times possibly easier. Even so, a day on a chalkstream is a great experience, and being fortunate enough to live close to both the Test and Itchen, I hope for many more.

Rods for dry fly are 8–9 feet long and carry a floating aircel size 5 to 7. Reels should suit the rod and have sufficient capacity to carry all the line, plus a modest amount of backing. Flies are specially tied to float and are then dressed with a waterproofing spray to keep them dry. By careful casting and delicate presentation the angler aims to keep his fly floating high and dry on the surface.

Rain-fed and Acid Rivers

In rivers and streams where fly hatches are sparse because of water colour, dramatic variations in flow, or the acid nature of the ground in the area where the water rises, the fish are often small. What they lack in size, they often make up for in quantity and because they are often hungry they take well. With only a very small part of their

Reservoir fishing for trout is one of the big growth areas in the angling scene

The end of the day. Some nice trout and a good chat about fishing

A happy angler with a good day's catch of trout from a reservoir

food comprising surface fly, wet fly is often more productive than dry. It depends on the day and the conditions. Even good conditions do not guarantee a hatch of fly, so matching the artificial to the natural may not be the prime need, but casting a dry fly into all the likely places will still bring results. At other times the wet fly fished either upstream or down and across is best. The variations are endless, as are the flies used. Local preferences are always worth following but as these change as the season progresses be prepared to listen and not automatically to use the fly that you used last time.

The tackle for rain-fed rivers is similar to that used on the chalkstreams, but because the fishing will vary from tiny streams to large rivers, rods will vary more, going from 7 feet to 9 feet 6 inches. Again a floating line, in sizes between 5 and 7, is used, but a slow sinker can also be useful. So long as the reel suits the rod and accommodates the line, plus a modest quantity of backing, nothing more is required. Again, many find an automatic reel has advantages because of the way that it eliminates slack – which is particularly important when you are casting upstream on a fast river. The automatic will get the slack up and on to the reel at a speed with which no ordinary single-action type can compare.

Trout fishing in high moorland water. River fishing for trout is increasingly difficult to obtain

An angler admires a rainbow trout taken on fly

Fishing in Fast Waters

Brian Watts

It is easy to understand how most coarse anglers derive a special thrill from 'fishing the stream', the art of trotting a float downriver under skilled control. On fast water, this calls for constant alertness, anticipation, and a very real understanding of what is happening below the smooth flowing surface.

It is my favourite form of fishing, fascinating and rewarding, sometimes dour but never dull. When choosing a venue for the weekend, whether match or pleasure fishing the call of streamy waters usually influences the decision.

The right gear is essential to derive full benefit and enjoyment from such fishing. So let's have a look at the tackle I select for

Fishing for chub on the Thames at Dodney Reach

such outings, and the reasons why. The delight of getting it right can so easily give way to angry frustration when the tackle does not perform properly, and this is almost always due to some miscalculation by the user.

Float fishing is the essence, the mainstay, of this form of piscatorial pursuit, so let's stick with this method – but take along a leger rod every trip so a switch can be made to leger gear on those days when fish refuse to take any but a static bait.

My rod, a fast tapered 'tippy' action type, of 13 feet length, three-piece, with the top section really two hollow glass lengths one spliced into the other to speed up the tip taper and keep all the action in the tip end, is checked before every trip. The High Bells stand-off rod rings can get knocked out of alignment. These rings keep the fine lines well clear of the rod to stop line-stick on wet days. A thin waxing of the rod helps it to repel water. Maybe it makes the rod a bit shiny in sunny weather but it does not really matter in this sort of fishing. It will not scare the fish. This fibre-glass rod was selected with weight in mind (less than an ounce a foot) and its good length of cork handle means I can tuck the butt comfortably under my armpit and still position the reel at the upper end of the cork section for easy handling with the other hand.

It is true that carbon fibre makes for much lighter rods. They have a grand strike and casting action, and have improved a lot over the last few years. They are still quite expensive, and some anglers have that lingering fear about their ability to conduct electricity and would not be caught out fishing in an electrical storm with them.

Two reels always go into the tackle box, sometimes three. Not much point, I think, in walking miles over rough country to a secluded swim only to have the reel pack up at the first cast, with no spare available and a long fishless walk back as the sole reward. Why a third reel? Well, two are of the closed face design, ideal for light line float trotting and virtually tangle free in the windy conditions so frequently encountered, and which so often leave lines draped round the handles of other designs of reels. The third reel is an open face conventional fixed spool type loaded with heavier line, just in case I need to switch to leger gear. Spare spools are included for both types, pre-loaded with various breaking strain lines. Slipping clutch mechanisms on all reels are checked to make sure they will let line off just before breaking point . . . and this may not always be at the strain attributed to the line by the makers! Sunlight degrades lines.

The waders, one size larger than shoe size to allow a thick pair of white fishermen's socks to be worn over normal socks for extra warmth, are taken from the garage wall where they have hung suspended by the feet since the last outing to prevent the rubber perishing, and the studs checked. These studs grip well on water-covered rock surfaces which more often than not are encased in slippery moss. Cleated bottomed waders are not a bad

alternative, and usually rather cheaper.

The tackle box is no larger than it needs to be. Terrain can be difficult and swims far from the road. But a small box needs careful packing: magapult, the disgorger, glare-beating polaroid glasses, float box, hooks, split shot and leger weights, quiver tip and two Northern-type maggot bags. Add groundbait and maggots, pack knotless landing and keepnets in the front and back pockets, and it makes up a formidable load, calling for a tackle box with a well anchored strap of strong material wide enough not to cut into the shoulder.

The rod holdall, with strong strap and base essentials, has extra pockets for the landing net extending handle, two banksticks, and an umbrella.

The fishing jacket, dull green/brown to merge with background and with wrap-over hood, and sleeves free of buttons and flaps round which line may tangle, has large pockets where Water Authority licences and club membership cards live. It was chosen with care, ensuring good overlap with wader tops so rain would not run down into them.

Maggots and casters, the freshly changed

Angling opposite boats and back gardens. The River Kennet at Reading

chrysalis of the maggot while it still sinks, are top baits for fast-water angling. The maggots must be heavy enough to sink easily, so ignore the smaller breeds like squats and pinkies. Good annatto-fed maggots are ideal. Casters need checking to make sure they have not developed air bubbles which will make them float. At least two pints will be needed for a day's pleasure fishing, more on some waters, and if you skimp here it could make a big difference to your final catch. Leave maggots in the sawdust added by your tackle dealer, but sieve off before use.

maggot, worm, bread and wasp grub are the only baits that really succeed.

So much for the tackle. Now what of the water. "Hold on", you say, and quite rightly, "just what do you call fast water?" Certainly, it's all relative, but I define it as 'living' water, lively flowing streamy water that bubbles over sills, chuckles around rock boulders, and ripples down glides. I mean streams, or rivers which are larger versions of the same streams. Many such waters are available to anglers in Britain, from the River Swale, which is the fastest falling river in England, and the fabulous

The tidal Thames at Teddington. These anglers are fishing for dace

Bread and punches. Bread will tempt fish in most parts of Britain

Brandling worms make a good backup bait acceptable to all fish, while bread, cheese, wheat, tares, hempseed, plus almost any insect, meat or edible fruit will tempt fish. On some rivers one bait may be favoured, while another is the success bait on a nearby water. If visiting a strange river, it is worth having a quick chat with a local tackle dealer, while a talk with a local angler will bring additional useful guidance. Anglers are a friendly breed, only too happy to give advice.

One thing about baits. The further north the river, the more spartan the fish diet becomes. On rivers on the Scottish border

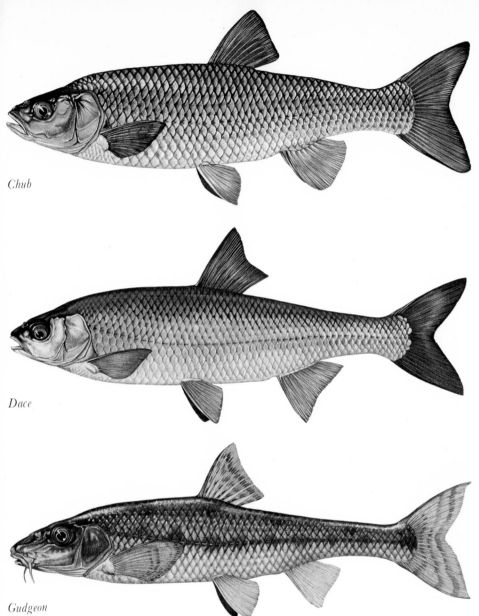

Chub

Dace

Gudgeon

but restricted Test, to the Wye in its beautiful border valley.

Let us imagine a typical swim. A grassy low bank gives way to sandy gravel at our feet where the clear shallow water laps. Upriver to our right is a slight bend and shallows easily waded, with the flow threading its numerous streams and swinging to the far bank, where trees overhang what looks like deep water. In front the sandy gravel slips deeper further out, the water a greeny haze, the flow fast on the far side. To our left downstream, 50 yards brings more shallows and a touch of broken water. The width could be 25 yards.

Wading is possible, to about 10 yards, just enough to obtain good float control but not scare the fish. They will retreat at our approach, warily, to the shelter of the far banks. There they will stay, and settle to feed if we take care. If they do become nervous, almost certainly they will just drop downstream a little way, but not beyond the lip of the shallows.

What fish can we expect from such a swim? If the river holds chub, dace, roach and gudgeon, all are likely to be present. Barbel and grayling, too. Bonus fish include perch and bream, though these species usually prefer quieter waters. The likely quarry must govern choice of tackle.

If barbel are known to be in the swim, we will set up with this hard fighting fish in mind. Once a bait is taken in its rubbery under-side mouth, and the hook drives home, this bottom-feeding bottom-hugging fish will use the full force of the flow to wedge itself on to the river bed. Or it may throw its full strength – and it could weigh up to 10 lb – into a sudden run down the current with a sheer burst of line smashing power. A 14 hook to 4 lb line is not too heavy.

It is more likely dace are expected. This means fine tackle: a closed face reel loaded with 2 lb breaking strain line to the correct level and with no knots in the line to create casting and trotting problems. The 18 hook is attached via 18 inches of $1\frac{1}{2}$ lb strain trace length. Shotting is simple, for starters, but be prepared to ring the changes if bites do not come in the first half hour. The float is an Avon-bodied type for stability and buoyancy, a stick float, or an antenna zoomer. The Avon is tops for control, ideal when the wind is blowing upriver. Shot is positioned from immediately below the float and spread evenly down to 18 inches above the hook – this swim may call for 5BB in total. The depth between float and hook is sufficient to allow the hook just to touch the river bed.

First get into position for a couple of 'proving' casts to check the tackle for casting ability, float setting, and depth. This means wading out – the float can be controlled much better from behind. Wading calls for care. Make sure all gear likely to be needed is to hand. Splashing backwards and forwards WILL eventually scare the fish. So arrange yourself as follows: sieved maggots in maggot bag around neck; disgorger on string around neck; the spare maggot bag holding extra floats, hooks, splitshot and magapult.

The keepnet attached to the bankstick can be wedged in your belt or down one leg of the waders. The landing net earns its keep as a 'feeler' for probing ahead on the river bed in murky water, a check on depth before each step. Then it can be stuck in the river bed next to you, handy for instant use. It is vital to avoid wading over deep gullies which can become traps with just a small rise of water level. Check the level on an easily seen rock or mark when you get into position – and get out quickly at any sign of it rising. A sudden appearance of floating dead leaves is a good indication of rising water level.

Having found a suitable spot to stand, with firm ground underfoot, water not too high up on the sides of thigh waders, anticipation builds. The first cast is always the most exciting. Dace can feed at any depth but it is better to get their heads down. Use loose feed, carpeting the bottom of the swim. The river is probably no more than five foot deep so fish kept deep are less likely to take fright. Groundbait may help, but start with just loose feed.

To take groundbait out when wading, use a smallish plastic box, mix up the groundbait with water from the river and stir in some maggots or casters. Place the plastic box inside the keepnet where it will float captive and easy to get at, and stop any big chub from leaping out of the net. No joke, it happened to me in a match, a two-pounder! Fast water fish are fit!

Decide where you want to pin down the fish, maybe a point several yards down river and well across, possibly right against the far bank. Cast upriver and find out how fast the water is flowing from the float speed. With this knowledge, and an idea of the depth, it is easy to guess where loose feed will land and carpet the bottom. Groundbait in tennis ball size mixed stiff falls faster and can be thrown almost to the spot, but use with care and not at all when the fish respond to loose feed alone. Groundbait can kill off a swim as well as bring reluctant fish on the feed.

Fishing against the far bank has its advantages. Fish are more confident at greater distance, will take the bait more positively and hold on longer. And the far bank is where any chub will be sheltering. Magapult feeding with maggots or caster will soon get them interested, but keep adding more loose feed every second time you cast the float in. The constant flow of food is a big stimulant to fish.

A chub bite is strong and certain. The float sinks steadily. The strike, and a hooked fish bores away. The first run slackens and the fish is turned by side pressure from the rod. Keep the rod tip well up, letting it do the work. Now bring the fish back – and get its head up out of the water. With its mouth out, the chub gives up completely and slides easily into the landing net. It could scale 3 – 4 lb.

Now for flashing silver dace, a fighter despite its small size, which in many rivers is a mere few ounces though it tops the pound mark in a few. The far North rivers probably offer more consistent sport with bigger dace; the Rivers Swale, Tees, Tyne, Eden, and suprisingly that queen of salmon rivers, the Tweed. The Scottish record dace was taken from this river at Coldstream in 1979 and even bigger specimens are present.

The dace is a shoal fish, never a loner. Catch one and you know there are many more not far away.

Trot for it. Cast slightly upriver again so the hookbait settles to the bottom just over the carpet of groundbait and the float sets itself deep ready to indicate the bite. The less of the float tip showing, the longer the fish will hold the bait, for it feels little resistance to arouse suspicion, allowing time for you to set the hook. Keep the line tight but allow it to play off the spool so there is no drag on the float – it flows with the current and at exactly the same speed. The bite will be fast, the hook set by a quick lift of the rod tip. Now move – fast! That fish must be moved out of the swim and away from the rest of the shoal quickly before its panic signals are picked up by them and they scatter. Now the keepnet shows its worth. Slipping fish back into the swim sooner or later leads to fear affecting the shoal and bites tail off to nothing.

If the fish start moving downstream, and you have to trot a little further down each swim before a bite comes, do not worry. The fish are not scared, but you are putting in too much loose feed and they are chasing bait drifting past them. Ease up on the loose feed and the fish will soon move back to where you want them.

Sometimes, despite all you do to get their heads down, dace insist on coming up for the bait. A change of tactics is then called for. Shotting needs to be altered so the hookbait sinks much slower, the depth brought up, and a lighter float may have to be substituted. Caster is probably more productive than maggot bait.

Switch to smaller shot, say No. 6, between hook and float, with any larger shot necessary to sink the float properly fixed straight under it. Trot down as before but let the line play off the spool between your fingers just slightly slower than the flow of the current. This checks the float and lets the hookbait go slightly ahead of it, so the fish see the bait first. It also allows you a fraction of a second more to hook the fish, necessary as the bite will be faster so high in the water.

Holding back hard, causing the hookbait to rise, sometimes attracts fish to the bait. They take it as it lifts, or prefer to wait until you release the line and the float dashes forward again allowing the bait to sink. This tactic can be tried when the fish lose interest in normally trotted baits.

Casting across the river into shallow water calls for practice, particularly over large distances. Shot positioning is important. Always have at least one shot more than halfway down from float to hook. This helps prevent the hook looping back over the float every cast. When fish really have their heads down, more shot can be moved down to give better tangle free casting and to get hookbait down quickly to the fish and increase the catch rate. It is possible at times to bunch all the shot 12 inches from the hook.

Sometimes bites are difficult to detect. One angler I spoke to on the river bank recently told me he had caught nothing, the fish were not feeding. No bites. In fact

An angler casting a long distance over fast running water

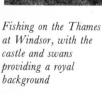

Fishing on the Thames at Windsor, with the castle and swans providing a royal background

the fish were taking his maggot hookbait every swim down but the only indication at the float was a slight lift, or sometimes a vague check in its progress. Strike on any movement or change, however small, sometimes more sensed than seen. If no fish results, nothing is lost, but it is surprising how often you are rewarded with a bucking rod.

Dragging bottom is another successful method for fast water dace. The idea is to let the float travel ahead of the hook. The hook is set a foot or more overdepth with the bottom shot just touching the bottom and acting like a drag anchor. It slows the hook to less than the current speed, frequently inducing a fish to take. The bite seems positive, a slow sinking float, but the strike has to be harder than usual to pick up

the extra line while the fish is still holding the bait. It takes practice, and some fish do pull loose or bounce off.

Grayling, another fast-water shoal fish, may be present in the swim, though this species insists on clean, well oxygenated water. Thus their retreat in the face of heavy pollution from the lower reaches of many rivers, to the still clean headwaters. They like gravel or sandy bedded swims 4–5 feet deep, in the main flow where food is brought down to them. The float and shotting set-up is as used for dace, though the hook is smaller – a size 18 or 20 – and set to keep just above the river bed.

Feeding routine with loose feed is the same. The bite is positive but the strike must be soft. This 'lady of the stream' has a very soft mouth. Unless the hook hits

behind the hard overlap at the corner of the mouth, a strong strike will almost certainly lead to a lost fish.

While maggots, and to a lesser degree casters, are good bait for grayling, there are times when they show a marked preference for the red and yellow ringed brandling worm. Loose maggot feed attracts them, but to score you must hookbait with the brandling on such days.

They fight hard, and with a peculiar 'spinning' twisting action which transmits up the line to the rod and immediately identifies a grayling hooked. The fish uses its unusually large dorsal fin fully erect to exert maximum power in its bid for freedom. With its soft mouth, and weighing anything up to 3 lb, it needs to be netted. Once landed, its full beauty is disclosed: a

bar of silver gray, with just a few black spots betraying its kinship to the trout. Handled, it gives off that very distinctive smell – crisp fresh cucumber!

Unless you intend to keep the grayling – and a very tasty meal it makes – return it quickly to the river. It is not a fish which will survive long in a keepnet.

Grayling are at their best in winter months, a fish willing to feed even after a hard night's frost has killed the appetite of other species. Dace do not like hard frosts, and seldom feed in such conditions. Chub are more likely to turn up in winter catches for they soon adjust to temperature drops.

The swim we looked at earlier is typical of fast-flowing rivers. Just as common are the upriver swims and small streams between narrow banks which run twisting

hollow glass eight-footer weighs only 6 oz and cost under £10, came ready fitted with threaded top ring to take bite indicators and is quite able to cast a 1½ oz spinner.

Care and quietness are a 'must' for small stream anglers. You are on top of the fish. Find a spot where you can get a clear cast downstream to where the water undercuts the bank in a bend and keep the float in the faster current right against the bank. Loose feed maggot or caster in a trickle into the bend. Set the float deep so just the tip shows – a small float, thin design to throw the minimum shadow on the stream bed, for fish shy away from moving shadows. Keep the shotting fine, No. 6 or dust shot, so the bait waves and darts naturally with the constantly changing flow. A few fish, maybe one good 'cup-winner', and it is time to move on in search of another holding spot.

One method which sometimes takes fish when the trotting tactics fail is the slow retrieve. No float is needed, just a double maggot baited hook with two BB shot nipped on the line 12 inches above. Cast downstream, and reel back very slowly. The fish hook themselves snatching at the bait, which I am sure they see as a freshwater shrimp. For this reason, white maggots are preferred.

Now let us look at another type of fishery: a section of wide river which, at first glance, is a mass of boulders and very little clear water, downriver along a straight until half a mile away it sweeps off into a left hand bend.

A closer look will show there are pools between the boulder outcrops, and in places these can be quite deep: dangerous wading water. Studied closely, we find there are plenty of clear areas where the main stream finds its way, a channel where the flow has etched its course over many years and where the river bed will be more even. These are the places to fish. Sometimes the main flow is near to our bank, at others far across.

Let's choose a spot where the main flow is well out, over an expanse of still water which is obviously deeper. Difficult to fish, it could be productive for dace and there is little chance of scaring them at such range.

Wading will only get us clear of the bank with increased freedom to cast without snagging undergrowth, but not enough to get behind the float for full control. That dead water will pull it back, even take it off

Top *Angling from a boat on the River Avon, with the pretty houses and bridges at Christchurch in the background*

Above *Fishing under the weir at Mapledurham on the River Thames*

and shallow under arches of overhanging trees. These are often very productive, holding a big head of fish due to the large volume of food available.

Such streams are common in the Yorkshire Dales and Vale of York, which hold many happy memories for me. The 'Vales' streams in particular offer challenging sport with grayling, with day permits for visiting anglers. For such waters, tackle needs to be reduced to a minimum. Throw away the TV angling image of a sleepy angler dozing on river bank – for this is hard fishing work and calls for some degree of physical fitness. A tackle bag is better than a box, and the rod holdall best left behind. The leger rod comes into its own here, but with float gear. Several useful short rods, say about 8 feet, can be had which adapt well for spinning, legering and shallow water float work. My two-piece

course and out of the main flow. So we choose a full bodied Avon float, one which is going to take more shot than needed to cast the distance. The extra weight is a big help in defeating the 'drag' of the line lying in the dead water.

Start with the split shot nipped onto the line evenly spaced from below float to 12 inches above hook, using the soft putty-type shot to avoid line damage. This swim may be about four feet deep, ideal if the bed is even. Cast to the far side of the main flow and let the float travel freely down – the line will soon form into an 'L' shape between rod and float as the still water exerts drag. Keep lifting rod tip to turn this more into a curved shape, the best you can hope for in the conditions. Strike on any movement of the float, with dace in mind.

So the bottom is snag-free, but some underwater boulders shallow the swim several yards down. Loose feed will accumulate at the base of these boulders, so this is where the fish will gather. Trot down again, hookbait just touching bottom. Approaching the boulders, check slightly allowing the hook to lift a little. Right on the boulders, hold back hard stopping all line playing out and the hook lifts over the obstruction. Then let it go free again to drop the hook behind where fish may be sheltering. No result. So set the hook about 12 inches over depth, bottom shot just touching bottom, and add an extra shot right next to it. Cast downstream into the flow slightly above the boulders. As the float sets, hold back hard so the hook swings downstream and lies just at the foot of the first boulders amongst the loose feed. Hold in this 'lying-on' position as long as possible, keeping the bait where the fish must be, though the line-drag will eventually swing the tackle shorewards.

Groundbait can be used successfully on this sort of swim. But again try loose feed first, and keep off groundbait if the fish keep coming.

Fast-water fishing has several problems peculiar to such angling. Sudden flooding, difficult wading, shallow waters, long casting are all part of the scene and these are overcome with a sense of achievement. Such water though is perfect for the canoeist, and where the water is so shallow just one canoe ploughing through a pre-baited swim scatters fish shoals. Time and more costly loose feed and groundbait are needed to tempt them slowly back again.

Many canoe people try to help, by swinging right over to the far bank and well away from you, unaware that they are moving right into the area to which you are casting. When wading, I can sometimes signal to them to pass behind me – or at worst just in front of me – where neither their sport or mine is spoiled.

Watch out for the odd trout while fishing the streams. Inevitably, you will hook into trout for this is their sort of water too. Many a good trout has been landed by dace anglers using light tackle – and several have been lost leaving snapped line as the only evidence of their passing. This is a vital reason for making sure the slipping clutch on the spool is correctly set – it is too late once the fish is hooked. Set it by pulling until the line 'sings', and adjusting so it plays out at this point. It is equally as important to have the landing net set up before starting to fish, and to keep it handy all the time. No point leaving it 200 yards away as you edge downstream trying different swims – then hooking a big one!

Sometimes it does happen. If it is a barbel your only chance is to slide it onto sand or gravel sloping gently, almost flat, into the water. With a chub there is no real

A fine catch taken from a rowing boat on the Dorset Stour at Wimborne

problem. Keep its head up, its mouth clear of the water, and you can bring it alongside you. Left hand behind its head, a finger gently into each gill, and it lifts easily and without struggle from the water. Handle with care so no gill damage occurs.

Legering in fast water calls for many different types of leger weight. The swim-feeder is useful, but the loss rate can be great. It all depends on the nature of the

Tree or bush 'cover' on the bankside is a bonus for 'floating caster' fishing for the fish can see you if you are too close to them and skylined. And distance casting is usually not possible because the tackle is so light – and a hard cast is likely to strip the caster off the hook. If the float catches up on a snag downstream, snap off and tackle up again leaving it to be recovered later after the swim has been fished out. Immediate

Fishing for dace above the Bell Weir lock on the River Thames

river bed. In areas where the river bottom is badly uneven, shallow, and with rough rock, a barrel lead drilled end to end and stopped 12 inches from the hook with a BB shot is best. On clear gravel an Arlesley Bomb is suitable, or a drilled round bullet lead if you want it to roll along the bottom 'stream searching' for fish – a good way of taking barbel!

Loose line fishing sometimes takes good fish. In high summer, a self-cocking float with no shot and a two-feet length to a hook baited with floating caster will take surface feeding fish eager for fly. Casting is difficult so try to get the wind behind you to help. Flick carefully onto the tail end of a pool, hold back the float until the caster floats at maximum distance in front of it, then let the float trot down holding back very slightly. A rise may signal a bite, more often you have to wait until the float gives warning. Do not strike. Stopping the line and holding is enough to set the hook – but the fish will probably boil on the surface as the hook pricks home and can bounce free! This 'boiling' only allows you to take a few fish 'off the top' before the rest take off in fear and you have to move on.

recovery could well scare the fish.

Using a fishing umbrella calls for an eye for good positioning, and a flair for the unusual. It is not always dry and sunny on the river, and standing out under a dripping tree getting wetter and wetter is no way to spend a day. The trick of keeping dry is to use the umbrella to full advantage. Bankfishing, you may be able to just stick it in the bank and sit on your tackle box. More likely not with fast-water fishing. Over-hanging trees can be useful when wading. Sling the fastening lines from the top of the umbrella over one and let it hang like a parachute. Always carry spare nylon string so you can reinforce its moorings in strong winds, extending to tree trunks if necessary.

Finally, on any trip to the river, do not forget your licence and permit or club card, and do not leave them in the car glove compartment for it can lead to a long walk back with an unconvinced bailiff to show him you do have the necessary authorisation. In the Yorkshire area this is particularly important, for having a licence is not enough – you must have it with you at the waterside or risk prosecution.

Still and Slow Water Fishing

Ken Whitehead

Like many still-water fishermen I started my career on the banks of a small farm pond using a six-feet bamboo cane for a rod, carpet thread for line and a round, red-topped bob-float with hook to gut (silkworm gut, liable to break without warning) more years ago than I care to remember. The tiny crucian carp that swallowed my bait were swung out of the water and dropped into an old zinc bath where they were kept till the end of the day so that I could gloat over them. Then they were gently returned.

Since those early days I have fished on rivers of every sort and size for every conceivable type of fish that swims, but I always return to that early love of still waters when the chance presents itself. In fact if I was given the choice of fishing the very best river in the country and that small pond, I would choose to try for those stunted crucians again.

Of course it is the utter peace and complete simplicity surrounding the still water scene that makes a magic of its own. No constant casting or re-casting to swim the stream, no worries whether the fish are there in the particular spot you are fishing, or a mile up or downstream. Even boats and bankside trampers are absent leaving you, the fish, and a chance to relax.

Mind you it would be wrong to say that I have always relaxed and enjoyed my fishing. And this could be said of a good

A well organised angler with his gear laid out within easy reach

A superb catch of roach and bream taken at Enniskillen, Northern Ireland

which perhaps you have suffered at times. Is there a cure? I can assure you that there is one, but it needs a great deal of perserverance, together with self analysis, and some careful forward planning and preparation, to effect it. Start with that business of moving from swim to swim in an effort to find the fish. It's largely produced by the man with the rod fishing where he thinks that they are, a decision usually based on casual observation made on arrival at the bank. As a hunch that type of selection pays off on occasion, but more often it is the forerunner to a complete blank.

Try some closed-season planning to beat this particular form of insecurity. Start by realising that to learn every inch of one fishery is difficult – to learn the secrets of half a dozen waters is nigh-on impossible. Study the track record of the various waters you use in terms of numbers and size of fish caught for the preceeding season or two, then decide on the one which produced the best results and holds greatest appeal.

Visit it at odd intervals and study it carefully. Map the banks, noting overhanging trees that have shed their leaves into the water over the years so that you can avoid those areas of rotting slime. Note the weed beds and any visible obstructions, then plumb the depth in as many places as possible, charting the measurements until a comprehensive picture of the underwater bed can be built up. When the task is complete you will be surprised at the number of new swims which can be discovered by reference to this rough map well before the season starts.

What about making your own swim? A number of angling books rave about this method and the sight of burly anglers dragging great rakes through weed beds is a common sight. My advice is to forget it. If you are fortunate and own your own water then it is fine – but you can bet that the swim you have cleared on a ticket fishery will have been occupied by some sharp-eyed angler every time you intend to use it. No, better by far to study your map and try to work out a swim that is unknown. If there are snags around it, then at least you will have the benefit of knowing where they are.

The same reasoning applies to pre-baiting. If you can be sure of getting the swim that has been prepared on the day you fish, all well and good. But if you

many other anglers that I have noticed, especially in recent years. They appear to be suffering from an affliction that struck me early in my youth called the Stillwater Disease, a subspecies of the dreaded Fisherman's Pox. It is an ailment that breeds on insecurity and worry, fed by recurrent blank days and mental aberrations connected with the use of wrong tackle and useless baits in fishless waters.

The net result is something that I am sure you have all seen – an afflicted angler staggering under a weight of fishing tackle guaranteed to produce a double rupture. He heaves this mountain of fondly-believed necessities around the bank throughout the day from swim to swim, often moving before there has been a chance of success until finally he heads back to the car, where vast maps are carefully studied in search of a different water.

So much for the affliction, one which I am sure you have noticed – or worse, from

cannot, you finish up with what you imagine to be second best, worrying what success the other chap might have in the swim you should be fishing. Whilst on the subject of groundbaiting, think carefully before you prepare a hundredweight or so for use on the actual day. Odds-on chances are that the eruption caused by its distribution when you first arrive will scare every fish away for the day, whilst the little-and-often approach of two or three handfuls generally advocated will only provide constant disturbance. A small offering in the palm of the hand, perhaps five or six pellets of paste, is quieter, can be repeated frequently, and will be equally effective if a good swim has been chosen. If maggots or worms are being fished close to the bank and there are shoals of small fish around, use a bait layer. Gently lowered to the bottom it will provide minimum disturbance, and place the bait exactly where it is needed.

So much for planning. Now for a little preparation – and the natural follow-on to groundbait is the hookbait. As a boy I had a secret bait, the recipe carefully guarded and the packet it was held in kept in my pocket away from prying eyes. The ingredients of this killing bait (yes, I caught a good few fish with it) were flour, water and custard powder mixed into a thick dough. Nothing new in that? You are quite right. But the important fact was that I firmly believed it was a killer, and my unswerving faith in its success increased my concentration out of all belief. Not for one moment did I wonder if I would get a bite. It was a case of when I got one.

The same applies to any fresh-water hookbait. Faith is everything, faith coupled with careful preparation. Of course the vast majority of still-water fish favour bread in one form or other, but that does not rule out success from baits that may be considered utterly outlandish. As an instance I have had some cracking days on a certain water where the groundbait was blood, about a gallon of it from the local abattoir, mixed and stiffened with breadcrumbs. The hookbait was bread moulded in pure blood, and I have landed vast nets of tench that had been suicidal for the stuff. A first-rate example of the unusual being successful – but I had to have faith in its ability to catch fish; it produced a blank on the first two days that it was used.

I am sure that a large amount of

Three nice bream, a popular fish for anglers in slow rivers and lakes all over Britain

Getting after the pike amongst the reeds from a boat

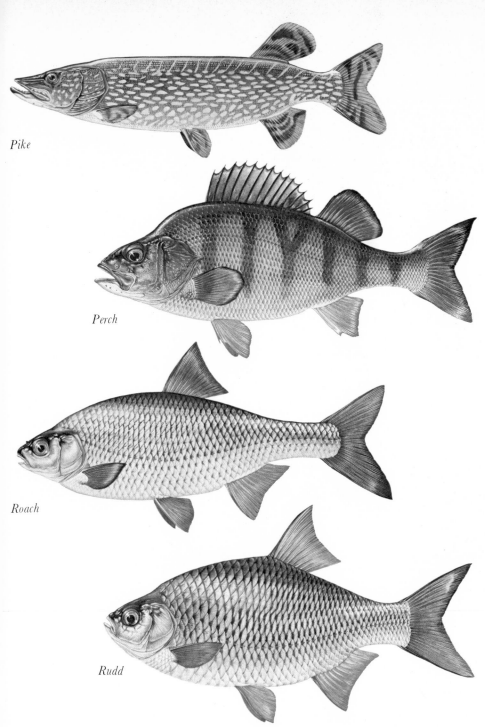

Pike

Perch

Roach

Rudd

Opposite *An angler tries his luck in an overgrown canal, framed by the overgrown canal bridge*

Left *A selection of coarse fish from slow-running or still water*

indecision extending into present day angling is concerned with the best rod and reel to use. Which is not surprising when you look at the vast array displayed in any angling store, each labelled by its manufacturer as being the only one that will cast a bait, let alone catch a fish. Well, there is one cast-iron fact where still water – or any other sort – of fishing is practised. You can fish with a battery of rods set out side by side, but if all of them register a bite at the same moment, then only one of them can be used to hook, play and land a fish. Now that is a pretty sure argument for the one-rod syndrome, and to further support the case is the fact that the man who uses one rod only can devote his whole time to watching it. There can be no divided

A battery of carp rods and bite alarms for ambitious anglers for whom one rod at a time isn't enough

Plenty of cover for this lake-side angler

chub it is an 11 feet Avon type. Both have a different action, but I cannot think of a style of fishing that they will not handle, and either one is capable of dealing with the exceptional heavy-weight we all hope will turn up.

The angling world has never been more fortunate in the choice of reels available on the market. Most selection lies in the fixed spool range, with good quality ball-bearing models that incorporate a roller bearing at the pick-up available for very moderate prices. Given a regular clean and maintenance in the form of a light oiling they are capable of lasting a lifetime. I demand one small refinement, and that is the tension adjustment placed behind the pick-up spool where I can alter it whilst a fish is being played, without sticking my fingers into a running line to reach the tension nut. But if you feel uneasy with the fixed spool reel, and more especially if you are one of those anglers who favour fishing close to the bank, take a good look at the old fashioned centrepin models. You will not be alone if you make one a choice – many top carp anglers favour their utter simplicity and swear by their inability to impart kink of any sort onto the line.

The hardest piece of self-analysis that I have ever performed took place on the day I spread out my tackle box and asked myself why I carried each item, whether it was really useful when I fished, and whether it could be of any possible use in the future. Those questions produced some interesting results; for instance there was a thermometer that I carried and occasionally used. Even if the water was below zero or near boiling point I would still want to fish once I had reached the bank – and as I would not know what the temperature was until I had arrived, it was the first piece to be discarded.

Out of the 20 or so floats I carried I only ever used three of them, so even allowing for spares that meant fourteen of them could go. There was a fair sized box of shot, the contents of which were rock hard and cut the line, together with hooks of a pattern I had discarded years ago, leger leads and swim feeders purchased for some long-forgotten reason and in near mint condition. I also managed to get rid of the box-within-a-box habit simply by dividing the biggest with wooden strips and glue.

Eventually I managed to ease a great weight from my shoulder and an even

loyalty, no wandering up and down the bank to check two floats or bite indicators, and definitely no line tangles!

Which rod is best? Well, sit down and work out the species of fish you spend most of your time fishing for, and the style of fishing you favour the most. Add to this your personal preference of rod length, and you are well on the way to making a sensible choice. My own preference for carp and tench fishing is the Richard Walker carp rod, whilst for bream, rudd, roach and the odd occasions when I fish for

greater weight from my mind. Weight is a creeping menace that can become a nightmare in itself, and it tends to build up around what I call the 'optional extra' area; things that are really necessities, but which tend to attract frills. Seats are an example. Many people choose a big box-seat that can serve a dual purpose and there are excellent models on the market. But a lightweight haversack and well-made collapsible aluminium seat with a high back support is easier to manage and far more comfortable – the comfort derived soon repaying itself in terms of added concentration.

Most sensible anglers consider good rod rests a necessity and not an extra, and they certainly are, providing they are plain and simple. I have never worked out the necessity of using rod rests fitted with bait alarms and designed for night fishing during the hours of daylight, especially where one rod is being used and maximum concentration being given to it. Keepnets fall in the same category as far as I am concerned. They are difficult to carry and, worse still, to dry out after use. Any pleasure that contemplation of the total catch could bring is rapidly ruined by the sight of displaced scales and mesh marks across the nose and tail fins.

Above *Enthusiastic boys fishing from a canal lock. Keepnets can displace scales and mark fish, therefore always handle fish correctly and use fine mesh nets*

Slow moving rivers provide good all-the-year-round sport for the keen angler

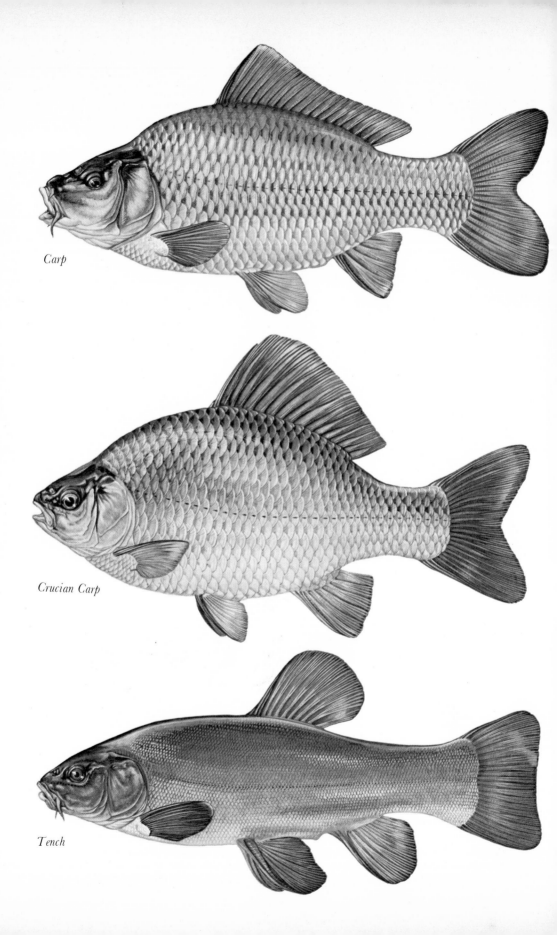

Carp

Crucian Carp

Tench

I shudder to think how many different angling rigs and styles have been evolved since the great masters of fishing, with names like Bickerdyke and William Senior passed on. There are scores of them, each with its own merit and useful in every type of water. So many in fact that one can spend hours reasoning out which style one should be using instead of doing that which is most important – concentrating on the rig already in the water. I am sure the size of water being fished plays a large part in this particular form of uncertainty, especially where large gravel pits and lakes are concerned.

For some unknown reason there is a tendency to believe that the biggest and best fish can only be found way out in the centre of big waters, so every bit of energy and concentration is devoted to throwing a bait as far away from the bank as is possible. Now, long distance fishing is fine, but it has three big disadvantages. It needs a fair amount of weight to carry a bait well away on a long cast, and that means disturbance when it falls out of the sky. It is far more difficult for a bite to be transferred from the hook to the rod through a long line, and finally there is no guarantee that the fish will always be out in the centre – they do move around. So to sum up; providing you have made a quiet approach to the swim, kept below the sky line, and used every bit of cover available, there is no reason to doubt that the fish can be caught at your feet, especially after a little sensible swim selection and groundbaiting.

Now that is not a direct attack on the leger rig which is most often used to carry a bait into distant parts. But it is a gentle reminder that the leger is a suitable weapon for close range work where it will

A young angler with a pike in his keepnet

Pierre Michels, former world professional coarse fishing champion, using a continental roach pole

Bickerdyke described its use at the turn of the century.

For most of my fishing I favour the use of a float. Not one of those match fishing monstrosities, but a tiny piece of peacock quill or a thin stick fashioned from elder-berry pith. Fastened by the bottom end only, it responds to the slightest touch when laying-on or fishing the one-shot lift rig, surely the most deadly method of float angling ever devised.

One final style must be mentioned, well known to the carp man but sadly neglected by many other anglers who rarely exploit its full potential. Free lining has been the style above all others used for surface feeding carp, the weight of a dunked crust allowing casts to be made over a reasonable range. Of course it will also account for good rudd – and I have caught tench on more than one occasion whilst using it in shallow water, close to reed beds. Of course it serves equally well as a leger rig – you do not have to fit lead onto a line before you can get a bait on the bottom – using a large hook and suitable sized ball of paste.

It is the mid-winter strata which is sadly neglected by still-water anglers, and slow-sinking bait used on a free line principle can be a winner in those regions. Try it on those static lowland rivers where thick-headed chub prowl near weedbeds under overhanging trees, on the lookout for food. Slide a fat black or brown slug onto a large sliced hook (one with barbs forged into its shank designed to stop the bait from working free), flick it out and watch for a hard take as it slowly sails below the surface. Even if you miscast and land in the weedbeds your chance of getting tangled are remote using this simple rig.

It is no exaggeration to state that the bulk of still-water anglers are round-the-year men, many of them concentrating solely on pike and perch fishing once the cold weather commences. Strange, 'winter is the only time for pike' attitude. There is the same amount of fight in a pike taken during July and August as in a fish caught during winter time, and they are equally keen to take a bait. A few tackle problems may arise where an energetic livebait is allowed to work close to weed-beds, and the spinning man has to wait for an early frost before he can really work a bait, but even those risks can prove worth-while in terms of reward.

Usually the pike man is an angler

be sensitive and accurate. Naturally the Arlesley bomb leger lead is synonymous with legering, and thousands are used and abused (yes, that little swivel in its neck needs oiling) each year. But for pure simplicity and practical use the pierced bullet is cheaper, and equally efficient. This round lead is held by a stop shot 18 inches or so above the hook, and it can also be used as a bait layer where short casts are made. Instead of loading loose cereal groundbait into the area of the swim, squeeze it around the bullet in a firm cup, then gently swing it out onto the bottom. In a short time the water will soften and lift that groundbait from the lead, leaving it just where it is needed – near the hook. A new innovation? Definitely not –

confident with his tackle and convinced that if a fish is going to feed, it will be certain to take the live or deadbait he is offering. In fact a great deal of tackle employed in summer fishing for carp easily doubles for winter work, with rods, reels, lines and the landing net playing a dual role. But the man who is prepared to spend a little money and invest in a second outfit will get the most from his winter sport. Spinning and plug fishing usually takes a back seat in the pike scene, relegated to a fill-in method to be used when nothing else has moved a fish, or perhaps when the supply of bait has been exhausted. This is a great pity, for both are rewarding sports in their own right, and the old piker's tales of small fish being the only ones to fall to a spinner should be taken with the proverbial pinch of salt.

To get the most from fishing an artificial lure you must appreciate that it is an aggressive style. Rather than cast out a natural bait and then wait for a return, you are going to attack a pike in its lair by throwing the bait close to it, then work it through its field of vision in such a way that it just cannot be refused. Although there is probably no desire on the part of the pike to feed, he will be made to feel that he must take a lunge at that challenging morsel.

Now that attack will only be successful if the rod is capable of casting accurately and retrieving correctly. Most of those that are sold are far too short, a legacy of the American system of spin fishing which crept into Britain some 30 years or so ago. Short rods are ideal for short casts on small waters, especially those that are hedged round with trees and bushes making a good swing and follow through on the cast impossible. But the average water, large ponds, small lakes and canals, will be better fished with a rod of eight feet minimum length, and for large lakes and gravel pits one of ten feet is near to the correct size. Not that the length or strength of rod bears any connection to a necessity for long casts – merely that the longer rod is better able to control the bait and a big fish once it is hooked.

One danger lurks whilst you are spinning; one small, constant weakness that increases unnoticed until the damage is done and a fish breaks away. It is called line kink, caused by poor or indifferent swivels between the line and the spinner itself, allowing the revolving bait to impart

Above *An armful of pike. A fine 28 lb fish caught in a gravel pit fishery in Surrey*

Left *A netful of smaller fish. Roach and perch provide good sport for anglers*

a fatal twist. There is only one prevention, and that is to invest good money in ball-bearing swivels, and then to see that they are kept free from ingrained weed and grit, with a regular touch of oil to guarantee free running. The use of an anti-kink vane, especially those small plastic fins that clip onto the swivel, also help to keep kink at bay.

I doubt whether the old adage that spinners and plugs catch fishermen and not fish holds good today. When tackle was cheap it was very easy to fall for an attractively painted or well-shaped artificial that one thought would be fun to experiment with. But present day prices have certainly put paid to that. The best spinners are those that revolve slowly and distinctly. and include spoons, bar spoons and leaf spinners. Choose plain colours and avoid pretty spots, stripes and painted faces; tests in a flume tank have proved that once the spinner revolves they cannot be distinguished.

Exactly the same advice applies to plugs. Slow-sinking, deep-divers are among the best providing that the water they will be

Above *Anglers making the best of difficult conditions*

Right *Pike fishermen skirting the edge of a large lake after their quarry*

used in has a reasonable depth. If the water is heavily obstructed, look for a floating-diver that will rise to the surface and float once the retrieve is stopped, allowing it to be eased over snags.

Fishing an artificial bait is not achieved by a nonchalant chuck and chance cast. As the bait fisherman carefully chooses a swim, so the man who spins should select the place to work his lure. A clear picture of underwater weedbeds – even though they have died down after the frosts – is a help, together with knowledge of sudden underwater troughs or steep shelves, something common in gravel pit beds and a sure place for a pike to lie. Alongside the bank, close

to the reed mace and rushes that line them, is another good place, and that includes the bank on which you are fishing, not merely the one in the distance.

Even if you are a died-in-the-wool one rod man, do not hesitate to spin. Take the float off that deadbait rig, set the hook into the bait so that there is a curve in its tail, and work it slowly back through the water in short sweeps, allowing a pause every now and again so that the bait will swing and sink before moving on again. It is one of the most killing movements in the spinner's library of bait working, and often accounts for the biggest fish.

Above all else, and regardless of whether

Top left *A deadbait rig for pike*

Top right *A selection of plugs for catching pike*

Above *A tackle basket makes a sturdy seat*

you are set for a day on a magnificent carp lake, or will be having to fight tooth and nail to catch a fish of any sort on one of those fisheries that seem to be blessed with more anglers than fish, relax. Relaxation is the most important ingredient in still-water fishing, and breeds confidence, aids concentration, and helps keep a cool head

when the big moment arrives and a big fish is being played to the net.

Travel light – two of the top anglers in the carp and pike fishing field that I know settle for one rod and a small haversack – and relax with the simplicity of your tackle. It's the key to success in the best branch of a great sport – fishing in still waters.

Fishing from the Sea Shore

John Holden

The time to begin shore fishing is autumn when the annual migration of whiting and early codling arrive in British inshore waters. These species account for the bulk of fish caught by shore anglers; they're easy to hook and you can find them almost anywhere on the coastline.

Autumn whiting can be so ravenous and prolific that you can almost guarantee catching at least a few even if you've never cast a line before. That is an important consideration because you need to land a fish or two very early in your angling career, otherwise you might be disillusioned with the sport long before you have had time to form a true opinion. Hook a dozen whiting on your first trip to the sea, and shore fishing will hook you.

Whiting shoals invade British beaches from the middle of September onwards. They are small relatives of the cod – a two pounder is a real prize – but what they lack in weight and power, they make up for in sheer numbers. When the season hits a peak, around mid-October, there are whiting to be caught on nearly every beach on the eastern seaboard of Britain and on the west coasts too. Imagine how many fish there are when, as the tide floods towards high water, everyone begins to hook whiting by the score. At the same time as you are hauling in fish, so are thousands of other anglers from Dungeness to the Tyne. Sometimes it seems that the bed of the North Sea is paved with fish. Their numbers must be astronomic.

As far as beginners are concerned, the importance of whiting is their utter predictability. Compared to, say, bass which make great demands on the fisherman's time and expertise, whiting are remarkably cooperative. You seldom need to single out a specific area of beach; they are catholic in diet, and they haven't the least reluctance in rushing in to snatch a bait from even the worst prepared tackle. If the whiting are inshore, you'll find some exciting sport.

Unlike some of the more timid, rarer species, the whiting is not too fussy about the stage of the tide at which it feeds. It is generally held that most fish reach the peak of their activity at certain stages of moon, tide and light level. Thornback rays are better lured near high tide on a moderate neap, at night after a thundery day. Early season whiting are nowhere near as fussy. They hit the bait in bright sunshine, in calm water, during a storm, on the ebb, flood or slack water. Of course, there are conditions that induce a mighty binge or even a total fast . . . but on the whole this is a species you can catch almost any time.

Plenty of angling activity from the beach at Lee-on-Solent

Whiting, an excellent fish for the novice beach angler, as in autumn in particular it begs to be caught

This feeding pattern is an aid to the newcomer because he will have enough trouble casting out and handling his new tackle in daylight. He will value not having to struggle in the dark. It is also far more pleasant to feel your way into shore fishing during late autumn when you are not frozen stiff by December winds and hail. These are small points that do not affect the experienced man, but they really do make all the difference between long term success and failure for the beginner.

All you need to worry about is tackle, for this is the key to not only making a start with whiting but also to being well prepared for other species that follow later in the angling year. The best way to choose tackle is to work backwards from the business end of the gear – the terminal rig that you cast into the sea. Here you will need only a simple one or two hook paternoster with hooks attached to 6 to 12 inch snoods of 15 lb nylon line. Your hooks can range from size 2 up to 4/0 for whiting, and although there are dozens of models on the market, nothing beats an Aberdeen eyed hook, which is needle-sharp, easy to tie on and adequately strong.

Make your paternoster in the following way (why not make up half a dozen at home . . . it saves time on the beach). Cut a three foot length of 35 lb nylon monofilament and tie a stand-off blood loop one foot in from each end. Blood knot a medium swivel to one free end of the line,

and a link swivel or plain split ring to the other. Attach a snooded hook to each stand-off loop, and there's your whiting rig. There are many, more complicated versions of the paternoster, but you can learn to tie them later on. This rig catches just as many whiting, and it's cheaper.

The size of the lead sinker you use has a tremendous effect on the overall strength of the line, rod and reel. The rod and reel must be matched to the sinker, never the other way around. Now, as most whiting prefer quite fast tidal currents, and because you will need to cast long distances into rough seas, a sinker of about 5 ounces is ideal. A plain bomb weight is useful when the tide is sluggish and you want the tackle to drift along the seabed. On the full ebb and flood you will need to anchor the tackle. Here we add anchor spikes to the sinker design so that it grips the sand and mud. To cover both possibilities, then, include both plain and wired bombs in your basic outfit. It's a good idea to buy a few 6 or even 8-ounce sinkers to cope with really rough conditions. And light ones – down to 2 ounces – add finesse to the sport in calm seas.

Next, let us consider the line. For most shore fishing, 15 lb breaking strain nylon is perfect. Load your reel properly and set the clutch to operate at the correct tension, and you will seldom if ever lose a fish because of the line's strength. But 15 lb line is no good for hard casting because it snaps under the

mid-cast pressure. To overcome this without resorting to heavy line all through, tie on about ten yards of heavy nylon to the end of the main line. A breaking strain of 35 lb is about right, though the more powerful casters use up to 55 lb.

This shock piece, or casting leader, is then tied to the swivel at the top of the paternoster rig, and its length is such that when you are ready to cast, there are still at least half a dozen coils of the leader remaining on the reel. That way, none of the casting force is transmitted to the thin reel line. But as soon as you release the reel,

Above *Fishing from rocks on the north coast of Cornwall*

Below *Beach fishing in Cornwall*

Sand eels are caught commercially for bait for beach fishing

Digging for lugworm and ragworm at Shoreham, Sussex. They make popular baits

I personally prefer a multiplier for most shore fishing. I find it much nicer to use, more precise and better matched to modern rods. However, a good reel costs close to £75, which is too much to spend unless you know that you are going to fish in ten years time. It is therefore a bad buy for the beginner, who, strangely enough, if he really wants to master the multiplier has no choice but to spend plenty of cash. The cheaper reels, though well made and long-casting, have no suitable casting controls. Only the sophisticated models like the Ambassadeurs offer easy casting . . . but the price is high. Certainly, a cheap reel that needs expert handling will be a nightmare for the learner.

The fixed-spool reel is therefore to be highly recommended. There are dozens of suitable reels on the market, but in my experience the beginner can do no better than invest in one of the medium-sized Mitchells, such as the 386 or 486. These simply cannot be beaten for performance, price, engineering standards and utter reliability.

Load line on to the reel until it is flush with the lip of the spool. Wind on the line evenly and tightly so that it settles neatly coil by coil. Nothing ruins fixed-spool casting so much as too little line laid loosely on the spool. That's a recipe for disaster. If anything, err on the generous side. Long distance men cram on every inch that the reel will accept.

And as far as distance casting is con-

the sinker pulls off light line, which has far less air resistance and therefore casts further. Casting leaders are standard equipment these days; you should always use one because it makes life far safer for the anglers around you.

For general beach fishing 200-250 yards of line are more than enough. This fits easily on to the smaller reels in the shore fishing range. With reel selection the newcomer reaches his first hurdle. Should he use a multiplier reel with its reputation for high-performance, but at the cost of birdnests? Or would a fixed-spool be better, though it might not cast so far or so sweetly?

cerned, do not believe that a fixed-spool is inferior. The fixed-spool record cast is 215 yards (1979 UKSF Finals), and the really good fisherman can approach 175 yards on the beach. In fact, the fixed-spool beats the multiplier hands down when the going gets rough. It is the king of headwinds, gales, speed fishing and rough-bottom clearance. Using a fixed-spool does not make you a second-class citizen; it is frequently the sign of commonsense.

Rod selection is a highly personal topic. It is unlikely that anyone can really guide you; you will not know which design suits you until you have had at least a couple of seasons' experience. Accept, therefore, that you will outgrow your first rod within a year or two. The answer, obviously is not to buy a very expensive specialist rod. These are often more difficult to cast and will not reach their peak unless you have a powerful advanced casting style anyway.

Look for an 11 to 12 feet rod, fine in the tip and stiff but not rigid in the butt. Go for plain hollow fibreglass, never carbon fibre, and concentrate your search in the 4 to 6 ounce casting range. Fittings are less important than the glass blank from which the rod is made. Hardchrome wire or aluminium-oxide lined bridge rings are fine; traditional screw-winch fittings or modern clips are satisfactory for holding the reel – the main consideration here is that the reel is fitted in the right place on the butt. For most casters, the reel is best set between 28 and 32 inches from the butt cap.

I would personally recommend one of the ABU Atlantic range such as the 464 and 484, the Bruce and Walker SX 406, and the lighter versions of the Daiwa Moonraker. Or you can build yourself a rod from a suitable blank in the Conoflex or Seamatch range. Many tackle dealers themselves build rods from those commercial blanks – so you may not have to do the whipping yourself if you do not want to.

Add a few spare sinkers and hooks, a sharp knife, spare reel spool loaded with line, extra leader material and a rod rest and you are ready to fish. Basically, whiting fishing technique is to cast out as far as you can – which will be 60 to 80 yards at first – with fresh mackerel or lugworm bait. Make sure the sinker anchors in the seabed if the tide's running, then prop the rod in the rod rest. When you see a bite – and you are most unlikely to miss seeing

King ragworm, irresistable to many sea fishes

one – pick up the rod, wind in the slack line and keep up the tension until the fish splashes ashore. It really is as easy as that! Afterwards, now that the fishing bug has bitten you hard, you can move on to learn better casting techniques. But with whiting fishing there is plenty of time to do that because they normally stay until at least mid-November by which time you will feel confident enough to tackle the cod as they appear.

Codding is a special world within itself, yet the basics are similar to those of whiting fishing. You will need to cast further, which entails practice in a field so that you can throw the sinker at least 120 yards every

A proud angler with an 11 lb 7 oz bass caught with crab bait on a 5/0 hook from Sandgate Beach, Kent

time. More especially, you will have to learn a great deal more about the seashore and the marine biology of the species you are after. Cod, though by no means a hard fish to lure, make more demands on your time because like most marine species they are on the decline. But you can be encouraged towards success by the mass of information available in books and magazines. More space has been devoted to cod than to any other species. In many ways it is the most important sport fish of the British Isles

From these beginnings, through a series of easy stages, you'll graduate to other forms of shore fishing. Surf bass, rock fishing, spinning, match fishing, pollack, wrasse, conger eel, rays, mullet . . . there's no end to the variations and special branches of shore fishing. But these options are open only if you understand what makes the sport tick. It is not a kind of fishing that tolerates the slapdash approach. The rewards are high, but the demands are beyond the chuck-and-chance fisherman's scope.

Like most dedicated shore anglers, I fish from the beaches and rocks because I cannot find the same enjoyment in other

branches of angling. Only the sea angler knows the wild freedom of cliffs and remote estuaries, of rolling Atlantic surf and windblown spray. Not for us the crowded inland waterways or the artificiality of reservoir trout.

Shore fishing is the only major growth area left in angling, and its survival is assured despite the continuing commercial drains on our oceans and inshore resources. There are fewer fish than there were even

Top *Fishing in commercial harbours can be colourful and rewarding*
Above *An unusual visitor caught at Mevagissey, Cornwall – an opah*
Opposite *Fishing from high on the rocks can be exhilarating but dangerous so take great care*

ten years ago; and now it takes a lot of hard work and deep thinking to succeed as a shore fisherman. Gone are the days when the dabbler hooked as many fish as the skilled man. On today's beaches, especially along the North Sea and Channel coasts, you must be expert in technique and tactics. Without the basic skills at your command, you may as well give up.

Paradoxically, the deterioration of fishing has proved the biggest attraction to those of us who fall under the spell of the seas. It is true that thousands of sea anglers turn elsewhere for their pleasures, but it is more relevant to judge the present and future of shore fishing by the number of men resolved to develop alternative systems that beat the shortage of prime fishing. This scientific approach itself attracts a yearly influx of beginners who revel in the sheer technology of the sport. In all, there is a massive undercurrent of thinking and determination that assures a bright future for saltwater angling.

The tackle market is primed to explode into a vast array of sophisticated rods, reels and accessories with a performace and sensitivity equalling that of freshwater and game equipment. We cast further than ever before. The British record distance cast made with standard rod and reel and the $5\frac{1}{4}$ ounce sinker is just one inch short of 240 yards. Pace that distance along the shoreline. It seems incredible that a glassfibre rod and multiplier reel, both available over the counter, could possibly hurl a chunk of lead that far.

Distances in excess of 200 yards are commonplace on the competition courts, but it is on the beach that distance casting makes its mark. A few months' practice, commonsense and decent tackle are the key to success. There is no reason why a man, woman or boy should fail to cast an easy 100 yards; 150 yards is nothing special. Indeed, modern tackle makes it difficult to cast *less* than 100 yards.

Long-range casting itself provides a stepping stone to better fishing. Why it does so remains a mystery; there is no cast-iron explanation of its power. But it is fact that if you cast your bait 100-150 yards you will hook more fish than the man who drops short of the 90 yard mark. It does not always work out like that: you can overcast at times. Through the years, though, the distance caster is top dog

It is interesting to compare our casting

tackle with that used abroad, for there is a clear link between casting expertise and the general standard of fishing. We have valuable lessons to learn perhaps. In America, where casting and fishing techniques with natural baits are rather mundane by our standards, short casts and mediocre tackle are deemed good enough, probably because the sport is better conserved than ours is. It compares with the superb cod fishing that singled out the mid and late 1960s as the shore angler's dream. You could hook literally hundredweights of fish without trying too hard and with the roughest outfits.

Change was forced upon us by the shortage of good sport. We think that poor fishing is specific to the British Isles, but that's not true. Consider what happens one stage further on in the destruction of the inshore fishing.

In Spain, along the Mediterranean coast, fishing grounds are so badly ravaged that our present stocks around the British

Isles seem marvellous. The Spanish angler's tackle reflects his frustration. In an effort to gain more distance and to present the bait with greater finesse, he uses line down to 4 lb breaking strain or less. Specially designed fixed-spool reels, aerodynamically superior sinkers and terminal tackle wring the last metre from the cast. Only that way, by casting maybe 200 yards with baits, can he hope to attract a fish. Success in those waters is measured in just one or two fish that fall victim to years of practice and dedication. It is no coincidence that tournament casting clubs flourish around such centres as Barcelona, where fishing prospects hit rock bottom.

The need for better tackle also results from a self-fuelling process. Those of us whose lives are dominated by shore fishing love to play with new ideas. The rods and reels we produce can also be of immense value for casting further and hooking more, bigger fish. Space-age materials like carbonfibre and advanced polymers begin to filter into the angling world. Good though glassfibre rods may be, carbonfibre offers greater design scope in all departments: power, weight, ease of handling, sensitivity, toughness and precision. In ten years time, perhaps sooner, quality fibreglass rods will be a rarity, having been almost entirely superseded by carbon. This material, supplemented by alloys and high-modulus synthetics, will spearhead the new wave.

Another factor boosts the march towards better tackle and more productive techniques. The name of the game is big-money match fishing.

It is not so long since sea match fishing was a bit of a joke. One or two events grew to assume a certain importance, but among the elite of shore anglers, match fishing was irrelevant. The more adventurous fishermen could not be bothered to fish for electric toasters and supermarket vouchers.

But cash speaks louder than silver cups and medals. When match organisers offered money prizes, the sea fraternity woke up. Five or six hundred pounds for a day's fishing is a powerful attraction. Add extra cash from the pools and you could pick up £1,000 for catching a couple of sizeable fish. Cash matches have eroded the old competition circuit that held sway for more years than anyone can recall. Where existing organisations cannot or will not conform to the new system, they are trampled on by new clubs and federations that represent the mass of anglers who are interested in fishing for money.

Yes it smacks of commercialism. But it provides the adrenalin necessary to kick shore fishing off its backside and into the 1980s. There will certainly be a direct spin-off equivalent to that which occurred in freshwater match fishing: new tackle and better methods of using it will grow in parallel to the number of big matches that are fished. Competition breeds innovation and expertise. The matchmen of the shoreline, like their riverbank counterparts, need every trick and device to ensure they stay on top. Money is the main inducement here, but it cannot be taken in isolation.

Large entries, lots of money at stake and a new outlook on the sport will produce sponsors. Sponsorship confers a certain authority on any sport, and this is reflected in media coverage, which in turn attracts more people into the sport. If saltwater matches continue to grow – bear in mind that major events attract over 2,000 entrants – television and national Press will take an interest. That, more than anything else, will consolidate the status of the sport.

The picture so far may suggest that British shore fishing is grey and rather dull, coloured only by competitions and technology. For the mass of anglers that is

The weigh-in after a beach fishing match. Matches are becoming increasingly popular

reality; but it need not be. There is a vast amount of work still left to do before we can claim to have exhausted all the possibilities that exist even in the British Isles. At the moment we cannot accurately measure remaining resources. There are thousands of miles of beaches, estuaries and rocks that are seldom if ever fished by rod and line.

On the coasts where commercial fishing is weak, shore fishing has its strongholds.

Add to that situation the normal ups and downs of migratory paths and breeding years, and you can see how easy it is for local beaches or even stretches of coastline to be without fish, if only temporarily.

Faced with these prospects, sea fishermen look further afield. That's why Ireland, Scotland and even foreign shores seem immensely attractive, as indeed they are. Of course, commercial fisherman work

A beach match at Seaton, Devon. Sponsorship for such matches could provide the inspiration for the future

Nothing denudes an inshore area of its sportfishing faster than trawling and netting do. Wherever overfishing has stripped the beaches of England in general, times are hard for the sea angler. The worst casualties are inflicted by gill nets, trammels and amateur trawls.

In practice, despite the rules that govern commercial work, inshore fishing is an indiscriminate killer of both mature and brood fish. Worst by far are the monofilament gill nets that can be set even on rough ground and over wrecks. Anglers have little or no protection from this onslaught, and they certainly have little recourse to law when their sport is wrecked.

the world, so you cannot avoid them entirely.

But shoreline environment can provide sanctuary, and some species of fish are not worth fishing for the market. Deep water, jagged rocks, jungles of weed and fierce currents rule out intensive commercial fishing of most kinds. But you can fish with rod and line into waters where the fish are seldom disturbed. There are still miles of this kind of fishing left in Britain, particularly in Scotland, the Channel Isles, even off the beaten track in Wales and the West Country. We simply are not aware of what sport exists; yet where surveys are carried out, the results are nearly always encouraging and often exciting.

Sea Fishing from Boats

Mike Millman

Boat fishing has four distinct aspects, each demanding a different approach, tackle and technique if consistent success with a wide range of species is to be enjoyed.

'Chuck it and chance it' methods have no place in modern day sport fishing. Unfortunately that message has not yet reached many who call themselves sea anglers, and among other things one constantly sees tackle being used that is out of all proportion to the size of fish likely to be contacted. We must, therefore, deal with each section in turn, to discover what constitutes balanced tackle and how it should be used.

Harbour and Tidal River

Harbour and tidal river fishing from dinghies and small craft is popular right around the British coastline. In most places it is possible to find a sheltered spot, even when a near gale is raging, and the expense is small after the craft has been acquired.

One should never under-estimate the fishing potential in shallow water as many species particularly bass, wrasse, thornbacks, flounder, plaice, dabs and at the other end of the size range, conger, are regularly taken, often to specimen weight.

Conger excepted, fishing for the species in shallow water calls for nothing more than a two-handed 8 to 10 feet spinning rod, matched with a skirted fixed spool reel or small multiplier, loaded with monofilament line. For flatties 10–15 lb breaking strain is quite sufficient, but it is wise to step up to 15 lb for bass and wrasse, and to 20 lb if the quarry is thornback and small-eyed ray.

In tidal rivers and harbour situations, all these fish can be caught by legering, but offering the right bait is vital to success.

Peeler and soft back crab dominate this type of fishing as crustaceans are a principal food source for fish that hunt inshore.

Peelers and softies are the common shore crab, in the process of moulting in order to grow, and then in the soft state while the new shell hardens, which normally takes about five days.

Boat anglers leaving the estuary of the River Arun at Littlehampton for a sea fishing competition

Running them a good second is live sand-eel, a bait that is rapidly gaining popularity due to the availability of battery operated air pumps, which keep them alive for long periods. Live sand-eel can now be purchased from commercial fishermen who specialise in catching them at many places along the English Channel coast. It is often necessary to make a return journey of perhaps a hundred miles to obtain a supply, but there is no doubt it will prove more than worthwhile. The cost of the operation can be quite reasonable if one man collects for half a dozen, the eels being decanted into separate containers at an agreed location.

When fishing with crab or deadbait it is customary for the boat to be at anchor, but with live sand-eel one has the choice of putting the killick down or drifting over a chosen piece of ground.

The latter is particularly deadly for bass, the eel being offered on a fine wire needle point 2/0 Aberdeen to a fairly long trace, which allows it to swim around in a natural manner. In this type of fishing, weight is kept to an absolute minimum, and a 1 oz ball or barrel is placed on the reel line above the swivel, which connects the trace. The rig is allowed to work about eighty yards away from the drifting boat and the rod is always held. A light multiplier is the best type of reel, as the line going away can be completely controlled. Bass hit a sand-eel hard and swiftly so it is essential to strike as quickly as possible if the fish is not going to be lost.

When the fish feels resistance it will immediately run off at great speed. If the slipping clutch on the multiplier is being used, all will be well. If not, it's goodbye bass!

Above *A 39-lb conger taken by Ed Schliffke at Cremyl*

Right *A fine undulate ray of about 12 lb being unhooked after being caught in Tralee Bay, Southern Ireland*

Inshore bass fishing is generally at its best in late October and November, when large numbers in the 4 to 8 lb range move in close to the land. The possibility of much larger specimens should not be discounted, however, as hardly a winter season goes by without at least a score of fish weighing upwards of 13 lb being reported.

Thornback ray are very much an inshore species and they like nothing better than the muddy bottom of a tidal river, which holds food in a thousand forms. This is a very strong fish and it uses its wing-spread most effectively to resist capture. When hooked from a boat it will immediately push its tail down and spread against the tide.

Ray have tough lips and tremendous crushing power in the jaw. When it finds a meal the fish settles down over it and the mouth, which is on the underside of the body, goes to work.

Oddly, peeler crab is the great bait for ray in South of England waters, but elsewhere mackerel or squid is just as good. It is usual to mount the bait on a 3/0 hook connected to a short trace of 30 lb monofilament or light wire, as it has to stand up to considerable rasping from the fish's mouth. A conventional leger rig is always used.

One should never strike what appears to be a thornback 'take' immediately. In all probability what is first detected is nothing more than the fish settling down, which naturally puts tension on the reel line, particularly if it happens to come out under a wing tip. It is always good policy to wait until a distinct movement is felt before any attempt is made to set the hook.

Baited spoon fishing from a drifting dinghy, which allows a lot of ground to be covered, is a fine way of contacting plaice, flounder and dabs, all of which are inquisitive species. Spoon rigs are invariably the brainchild of enthusiasts, who spend years developing the perfect blade for a particular area. Produced in brass, copper or plastic and depending on the subtleties of shape, spoons can be made to wobble, flutter or have an undulating action. Colour plays a big part. What is right in one place can be all wrong in another, so it is very much a question of trial and error. The conventional spoon is usually placed about six inches from a fine, size 1 or 1/0 hook, in such a way it will move freely when drawn through the water. A small

barrel lead gets it down to the bottom where it's allowed to work just above the mud. When doing so correctly the rod tip 'ticks' rhythmically. Every so often the spoon touches the bottom, raising a tiny cloud of mud particles, and it is this that often induces a flattie to attack the baited hook. Tidal rivers with sandbars, where there is a fair run of tide, are usually good places to try your luck. Spinning with a spoon from a dinghy anchored uptide of the banks is a much used method for flatties, which lie behind the bars waiting for the run of water to bring food their way.

At the word conger, most boat anglers immediately conjure up visions of gloomy wrecks lying in deep water far from land. True, that is where the multiple catches of outsize fish are made, but when it comes to individual giants, harbours and tidal rivers are quite capable of producing them.

Because they are nocturnal creatures, the best action is after dark, when the eels venture away from holes in rocky ground, crevices in harbour walls, the shelter afforded by old pipes and similar seabed flotsam.

Three well pleased fishermen after a day's sport pollack fishing at the Bishop Rock, Isles of Scilly

Shallow water conger fishing is merely a matter of anchoring over a likely spot and legering a good size mackerel or squid bait. Waiting is all part of the game, and one should not expect the first bites to come for at least an hour. Chances are, it will then be small slip conger that feed first. It is a traditional pattern that seldom varies.

Tackle for the rough 'hurly burly' that is conger fishing, is the same as one would use when fishing reefs in deep water offshore. This means a 20 to 30 lb class rod matched with a 4/0 multiplier and 35 to 40 lb breaking strain line. The 18 inch trace is of good quality wire to at least an 8/0 hook. A 4/0 swivel connects the trace to the reel line on which is run the weight, held by a sliding boom or simply a swivel, which is tied to it with light nylon. This method has distinct advantages. A swivel is much cheaper than a china eyed boom, and the weak nylon ensures that only the lead is lost should a hang-up occur, and it is usually that part of the rig that gets jammed in a crevice.

Conger traces made up in the workshop at home cost about 60p a time, so it's a worthwhile consideration.

There is absolutely no need to hold the rod as conger must be given plenty of time to take a bait down. In shallow water the largest fish can be shy feeders, and I have experienced fifty pounders that took a bait so gently, it was no easy task deciding the moment to strike.

It is good practice to hold the reel line between thumb and forefinger, as that is the most sensitive way of detecting what is going on down below. Once a definite series of pulls and jerks is felt the reel is put into gear and the slack line wound in. At this point the weight of the fish will come on to the rod, and then is the time to strike the hook home.

Now, the eel must be winched away from the bottom as quickly as possible as it will try to dive into a crevice and no amount of pulling will induce it to come out. Even a tail hold is extremely difficult to break, and the fish will allow itself to be skinned rather than let go.

Once the conger has been played to the side of the boat, a gaff must be used to get it aboard, but that only applies when dealing with fish weighing in excess of 15 lb. Smaller eels can be lifted over the gunwale undamaged and returned to the water. Unhooking any size conger should not be taken lightly as the jaws are capable of inflicting serious wounds.

When dealing with large fish it is best to unclip the trace and leave the fish well alone until it has had time to quieten down a little.

Night fishing should never be attempted without the aid of a good light. Much the best is the pressure type which will shine brightly for a long period at little cost. Needless to say it must be tied securely to a suitable object to prevent it being tipped over. It is also good sense to take along a couple of big sacks, as there is nothing worse than a large eel roaming loose in the bottom of a small boat.

Inshore Boat Fishing

We now move on to what can be termed inshore boat fishing, which is generally considered to take place within three miles of the land, but the sea even that short distance out can be a dangerous enemy. This category embraces the type of tackle, species and techniques already mentioned, but now can be added several more kinds of sporting fish and methods.

Whiting, pouting and dogfish will be found over muddy and shaly ground throughout much of the year, and can be caught with two or three hook paternosters baited with thin strips of mackerel and squid or marine worms. From late June until November red and black bream show up along the English Channel coast, and there is hardly a gamer species in the sea. Rocky ground gives up the greatest numbers, but to get the best of sport it is vital to fish with light tackle. Paternosters are much used, but there is nothing to touch a 10 lb breaking strain 3 ft trace to a size 1 or 1/0 hook. Top baits for both species of bream are squid and mackerel strip and both lug and king rag-worm.

Rocky outcrops with a minimum of five fathoms of water over them are the hunting ground of pollack. On inshore marks they average about 3 lb in weight, with a few touching double figures.

The best approach is to fish on the drift over a likely area, until the fish are contacted. After that, one has the choice of continually running over the spot, which should be marked with a small buoy, or fishing at anchor.

A good way of making a fine catch of inshore pollack is to use a long trace from a light plastic sea boom, which is weighted at one corner, but there must be a good run of water to work the bait in a natural manner. A drift line can also pay off, particularly in tide rips if one has live sand-eel for bait. Float fishing is also a deadly method. The technique is to let a seven-inch float drift away for at least a hundred yards, then retrieve it slowly. It is rigged as a slider with a 1 oz ball or barrel lead, so the bait can be made to swim at a desired level. King-rag and live sand-eel are usually the most successful bait in this type of fishing.

Trolling a bait, natural or artificial, behind a moving boat, has long been a favourite way of catching species such as

A big fish bends the rod off Stornoway, Outer Hebrides, Scotland

bass, pollack, mackerel and garfish.

It is impractical for more than four men to fish at the same time, so trolling is a game for anglers with their own boat. Baits are varied, ranging from live and dead sand-eel through mackerel and squid strip, to various types of artificial eel. The bait is offered on a long trace and worked from a 10 ft rod, with a semi-stiff action, outside the disturbance caused by the boat's propeller, which means at least 100 yards.

Trolling from a wooden boat gets better results than when fishing from a craft with a fibreglass hull. Sound is absorbed by wood, but goes straight through the more modern material.

The amount of weight to be used depends on the strength of the tide, speed of boat, and depth the bait is to be fished. The best types of trolling lead are those whose centre of gravity is below the level of the line, which prevents any suggestion of twisting and kinking. The curved jardine is mounted by running the reel line around a continuous groove, and spiral wires at the ends. It presents little or no resistance to water, and can be changed without cutting the line. When trolling the rod is held at all times, in readiness for the strike. Bass and pollack hit baits like lightning, so no time must be lost in striking the hook home and stopping the forward motion of the boat.

Coming back to trolling with dead eel, it is essential for the fish to move in a life-like manner, so it is bent backwards and forwards until its backbone is broken in a dozen places. Alternatively, a strip can be cut from the entire length of the eel, but it must have clean edges, the hook being passed through the thickest end.

Offshore trolling for outsize bass and pollack, at such places as the Eddystone Reef, which lies nine miles off the coast of Cornwall, provides thrilling sport for experts who have a thorough knowledge of the ground. Wonderful catches of very large fish are made on artificial eels worked just after first light and at dusk during spring tide periods. Fishing at first light resulted in the capture of the British record bass of 18 lb 6 oz by Roy Slater, in 1975. The run of a double figure fish is one of the most exciting experiences in sea angling, and such a specimen does not give up without a great fight.

Surface indication plays a big part in sea trolling. If a large flock of sea birds is seen wheeling and diving over the water, the chances are bass and pollack will be feeding on fry. A bait worked through the spot is likely to get a quick response.

Other renowned places for bass trolling include the Gwingeas Rock, which is close to Mevagissey, the Manacles Reef near Coverack, and along the coast of Cornwall between Penzance and Cape Cornwall.

Deep Water Reefs

Deep water reef and open ground fishing requires a sturdy boat at least 25 feet in length, equipped with life saving equipment for everyone aboard. There should also be a waterproof pack of flares. Personally, I would not go afloat offshore in

Below A pollack of over 24 lb caught from a wreck off the Cornish coast

Below right A fishing expedition setting off round the coastline

any boat no matter how good the weather, without these safety aids. Make no mistake, the sea is a merciless killer, and anyone who goes unprepared for trouble is taking a grave risk.

An echo sounder of the graph type is a tremendous asset for pin-pointing areas of rock, as it is over that sort of ground that one is likely to contact pollack, ling, cod, conger, turbot and bream. Tackle for reef fishing in deep water is usually 20 and 30 lb class boat rods matched with 4/0 multipliers with line up to 40 lb breaking strain, but there is a definite swing to lighter gear, and major manufacturers are now offering 12 and 15 lb class rods. This section of boat fishing can be done at anchor or on the drift. The former is certainly more popular, but it is essential to be in the right place.

Most species inhabiting a reef tend to stay on the leaward side of the main pinnacles or walls of rock, and that is particularly true when the tide is running hard. The boat must be anchored well uptide of the peaks, so that the baits clear the top and land where the fish are.

Most predatory species only feed when the tide is running. It is quite uncanny how a mark that seems devoid of life during the slack tide period comes alive with fish the minute the water starts to make.

The cream of coalfish and pollack fishing is found at such places as the Eddystone Reef, the legendary Hatt Rock, which lies ten and a half miles south of Polperro, and the Wolf Rock, nine miles out from the tip of Cornwall.

A visit to any one of them will result in plenty of fish to a weight of 16 lb, with the possibility of a 20 pounder.

Most deep reef pollack are found within 30 feet of the bottom, and are fished for with 'flying collar' rig. It is made up from an eight-inch French boom with split rings and swivels. The reel line is connected to the swivel at the top of the L, the trace ending in a 4/0 hook to the swivel at the long arm of the boom, and the weight holder at the angle of the L. Technique is to allow the boom to run to the bottom from where it is retrieved slowly through the first 60 feet of water, this procedure being repeated until the level the fish are feeding at is determined. Now, the bait can be worked in the productive zone, which saves a great deal of fishing time, consequently increasing the day's catch by a considerable amount.

The length of trace is entirely dependent on the run of tide. In spring tide conditions up to 25 feet is used by pollack experts, but during neaps, 10 – 15 feet is ample. The bait can be squid or mackerel strip, king rag-worm or an artificial eel, Eddystone and redgill models being most effective.

When pollack and coalfish take a bait they immediately make a tremendous power dive for the bottom which takes a line off the multiplier at an incredible speed. At all costs the fish must be allowed to run under pressure from the slipping clutch.

When the run stops, line is retrieved steadily with a pumping action, but the

An echo sounder used to locate underwater rocks, around which will be found many good sporting species

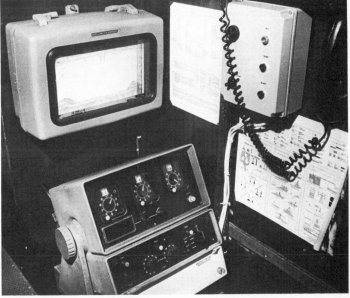

average double figure specimen will put in as many as five splendid dives before it can be worked to the surface.

Of the two species, the coalfish is the better fighter. It is a more compact fish than the pollack, and is to a great extent unaffected by quickly changing water pressure. Many a good coalie has escaped with a last desperate flick when the battle seemed won.

The flying collar rig can also be used for drift fishing, but it is customary to shorten the trace down to 10 feet.

Great banks of sand lying in deep water are the home of the turbot, plaice and brill. Traditionally they are fished for at the Skerries, Shambles, and Varne Banks, which lie off the English Channel coast, but sandy channels between areas of rock also produce excellent fish.

A noted example is the Manacles Reef, where turbot to a weight of 29 lb and plaice to 7 lb have been caught. On the open banks fishing on the drift is usual, but for working gullies an anchored-up concept is best, once the exact geography of the ground has been established.

Tackle for drift work is a 15 to 20-feet trace, worked off a weighted boom, with a second swivel four feet from the hook, which should not be smaller than 4/0.

It is a useful dodge to position a small barrel lead just behind this swivel, to take the bait back to the bottom very quickly after it has bounced over the top of a ridge.

This really pays off as many big flatties

lie half buried in the sand behind the banks in wait for a luckless fish to appear.

Hunting for blue, porbeagle and, to a lesser extent, mako and thresher shark, is a pastime enjoyed by an increasing number of anglers, and particularly so as a holiday or special excursion.

Cornwall is Britain's centre of shark fishing activity, principal ports being Looe and Padstow. The former has a fleet of some 30 boats, which make daily trips to the general drift area, 20 miles south of the coast. Blue sharks averaging about 50-60 lb are taken in large numbers, although there is some evidence of a decline in recent years.

One in a hundred is a fish of 80 lb, and in the course of a season which runs from June

A porbeagle shark comes aboard after being caught off the North Devon coast

Top *An angler battling with a monkfish*

Above *A monkfish being put back into the sea*

Right *A fine turbot and its captor*

to October, about a score in the 100-lb class are caught. The British record blue shark of 218 lb was taken off Looe in 1959, and it is possible the record will never be broken, as since that time only one other fish has topped the 200-lb mark and there have been only four weighing in excess of 170 lb.

Once in the area where sharks are likely to be, the skipper sets up a drift which is maintained throughout the day. Net bags full of rubby dubby, a nauseating mixture of pulped herring, mackerel, blood and fish guts are hung over the side of the boat at bow and stern. The oil seeping out creates a lane of attraction along which a hunting shark is drawn. It is customary to have four baits out suspended at different levels, from balloon or cork floats.

Nothing more than medium-weight tackle need be used, as once hooked the blue shark does nothing more than dash about in open water, and there is usually at least 200 feet of it beneath the keel. A 15-ft wire trace to a 10/0 hook is essential, as the shark's skin is rough enough to wear monofilament and braided line through in a short time. Whole mackerel or bunched herring is the common bait.

Although the occasional porbeagle is caught in South Cornish waters, Padstow on the north coast is the place to set off from if one is after that species.

Unlike blues, the much larger porbeagle hunts very close to land, and is occasionally hooked a few hundred yards out from vaulting cliffs and headlands, where there is a good run of tide.

The World and British record porbeagle of 465 lb, was fought off Crackington Haven, at times in less than 18 feet of water, and there have been numerous other heavyweight captures in identical circumstances.

Fishing for them is done on the drift but the concept differs in that the boat is maintained within a relatively small area. Dubby is used, but instead of a definite single slick going away, the oil spreads over a square mile or so of sea, thus creating a box of attraction.

Tackle is a 50 or 80-lb class rod with either a 6/0 or 9/0 multiplier, and line up to 100 lb. A very strong 12-ft trace swivelled at the mid-way point is essential to resist powerful jaws and the porbeagle's habit of rolling the wire around its body. The average weight of porbeagles caught off north Cornwall is close to 170 lb and fish of this size fight for the best part of an hour.

Porbeagles cannot be played in shallow water from a fighting chair, so it is tiring on arms, back and stomach, but then a little pain is good for the soul.

Wreck Fishing

Our final excursion is into the spectacular world of wreck fishing. This is a sport where you must have the services of a professional skipper, who operates a boat fitted with every conceiveable electronic aid for pinpointing not only the position of a wreck to within a few feet, but showing large individual fish swimming above the pile of junk. Anyone engaging in an offshore wreck fishing expedition must be prepared for a long tiring day at sea, and at the end of it, to carry away just two fish, no matter how many have been caught. 'Two fish only' is a hard and fast rule on most top flight deep water wreck charter boats, particularly those operating out of west country ports. It is a cardinal rule therefore, to check the terms of charter when you book a single fishing place or take the whole boat for a party. If you do not like the system of the skipper retaining most of the catch, it is a question of 'shopping around,' or taking a trip on a deep water reef boat where you keep all you catch. It is not a bit of good going on a wreck boat where a limit is imposed, and then bitterly complaining when you arrive back with half a ton of prime fish.

Skippers justify the regulation on the grounds that they need to sell the catch to defray the high cost of top-class rod and line fishing far offshore. Without it, the price of a day's charter would rise considerably.

Personally, I have always fished for sport, and not to fill the freezer. It is an attitude that has led me to many memorable days on wreck boats, as every skipper who keeps the catch makes sure he goes to a mark holding enough fish to keep a party of ten anglers busy throughout the day, It is as well to bear in mind that in wreck fishing 'two fish' can mean 40 lb of fillets.

Although many wrecks hold a large number of species, often in vast numbers, it must be firmly understood that to get good catches one must be prepared to work hard. Sitting on a fish box with the rod resting on the gunwale, waiting for the fish to jump on the hook, will just not do.

Most of the heavyweight catches are made up of conger and ling. There is

Above *Rubby dubby being released over the side to attract sharks*

Left *A full string of six mackerel on feathered hooks. Mackerel are often used as bait for bigger fish*

nothing delicate about the way these species feed and fight, so they should not be handled gently either. Both are essentially bottom huggers that immediately try to dive into the twisted wreckage after feeling the hook.

It is at this point the inexperienced angler loses the fish, having failed to pump like fury to get it away from the danger zone before it had time to realise what was going on.

To drag a 50-lb conger bodily requires a hollow glass rod in the 30 to 50-lb class,

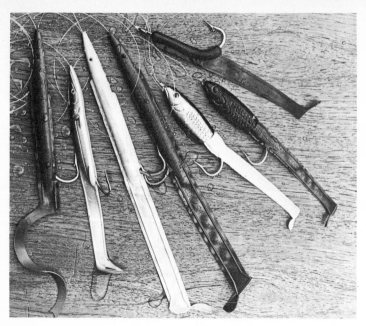

greater resistance to water demands the use of more lead.

Wire line is rapidly gaining popularity for deep-water fishing, especially in areas where there are fast tides, but it must be used intelligently if kinks are to be avoided.

With its small diameter, even in high breaking strains, wire line allows small leads to be used, which is a tremendous advantage in 40 fathoms of water.

A narrow metal spooled multiplier and aluminium oxide rod rings are essential.

Conger and ling traces must be of good quality wire fitted with a stout swivel, and a 10/0 hook, preferably an offset point pattern. Most specialists avoid nylon covered wire, and use cable-laid, which is sold by the metre at good tackle shops and ships' chandlers.

Mackerel and squid are the usual baits and they can be offered in a variety of ways. Whole mackerel is mounted with the aid of a baiting needle or presented with the backbone removed, from either the head or tail end. I rate squid very highly for conger, having caught 37 fish over 50 lb on it. The head and tentacles make great bait, while the body can be offered whole or cut in half.

Pollack and coalfish abound in wrecks, but as the tackle and flying collar tech-

Above *Artificial eels for sea fishing. Left to right: troller, thresher, two Eddystones, two coalies and a hunter*

Below *Deep sea anglers off the Shetland Isles*

matched with a 6/0 multiplier filled with the appropriate breaking strain line, which can be monofilament or braided dacron. It is a matter of personal choice which type is used. The stretch in monofilament is an in-built safety factor against the run of a big fish, but it makes positive striking difficult. Braided line does not stretch at all, but its

nique already described is exactly the same for wreck fishing, let us look at another way of taking them, and the cod, during winter months when the greatest number congregate on sunken hulks, and fishing is at its very best.

The rig is a two-hook paternoster, with either artificial eels or 8/0 hooks baited with strips of squid or mackerel. Weighted with at least a pound bomb and worked on the drift, it is allowed to plummet to the hulk, and then jigged as the boat passes over it.

Quite often both baits are grabbed simultaneously, as they near the bottom, which puts a high level of strain on the snoods, the fish swimming away from each other in a panic.

Heavy duty nylon monofilament of 80-lb or so breaking strain is used to make up the traces, and it is tied from a single length, which produces a double snood. To pass this thickness through the body of a conventional sized artificial eel, the nose has to be snipped off, but with very large

models developed recently, especially for this type of fishing, it is unnecessary.

Pirking is another way of fishing on the drift, but it requires a lot of physical effort, particularly with 24 to 30-oz lures.

For this game you need a longish rod with plenty of lifting power in the butt and a high geared multiplier.

An extension of the pirk, or jigger as it is also termed, is Eddystone's coalie lure. The largest model from a range of five has a 6-inch body made from lead, weighing $19\frac{1}{2}$ oz, and is plugged into a conventional PVC tail, which brings its overall length to 11 inches, a decent mouthful for any self-respecting predator.

Unlike the pirk, which is worked sink and draw, the coalie is dropped to the bottom and retrieved at high speed, which is essential if the tail is to work correctly.

No matter how good the design of an artificial eel, its success is totally dependent on movement. All have a negligible action of their own, and only that imparted to it by an angler gives it life.

A fine ling, a fish to be caught when wreck fishing

The Wandering Tope

Alan Wrangles

Tope! Here is a sprightly piscine nomad, who, it would seem, cares not a fig for convention, and can be as unpredictable as the element in which it lives.

Tope of 40, 50 or even 60 lb may be hooked in placid water only a few feet deep, or they may hit a bait lying in 20 fathoms of tidal race. But whether the water be deep or shallow, placid or tide-swept, the tope will seldom leave you in any doubt of its intentions, which is to put distance between it and you in the shortest possible time.

The rumbustuous rip-roaring way in which a tope will set a reel spinning during its first run has induced many an angler to become set in his ways, and devote the whole of his fishing energies to hunting them.

I can readily understand this attitude, but I must admit that it is not one to which I subscribe. I am, if you like, an angling philanderer, accepting gladly what each and every species has to offer, but neverthe-less, tope, salt water Cossacks, have for me always lived up to the promise held in their streamlined power-filled body.

As their shape implies, they are a member of a large group of fish, the sharks and dogfish, generally known as Selachii, the Cartilaginous fishes, as distinct from the class of bony fishes, Pisces.

Cartilaginous fish have a skeleton which is entirely tough gristle or cartilage. There is not a vestige of bone anywhere.

It is a quite large group of fish, ranging from skate and rays such as white skate, long-nosed skate and thornback ray, to the well known porbeagle and mako sharks. Dogfish also belong to this group, and appear in fishmongers and fried fish shops as possibly flake, huss or under other 'trade' names.

Tope are requin sharks, belonging to the family Carcharinidae, as do the infamous tiger, and far less notorious blue shark.

The former are known as man-eaters, but the blue, a frequent visitor to British waters, has no evil reputation.

In common with most fish, tope have a number of local names. These include penny dog, miller dog, sweet William, white hound, and in Wales some anglers refer to tope as 'blue dog.'

Unlike the deep bodied, much heavier porbeagle, tope are relatively slim species, with small gill slits and two dorsal fins, and are generally a greyish/brown shading to white on the belly. Other visible features include a short but deep notch in the lower lobe of the tail, small nostrils, and small spiracles, close and to the rear of each eye.

Their food consists mainly of other fish, particularly plaice, sole and dabs, but bream, wrasse, whiting, codlings, pout and indeed most other species that they can catch will be eaten. Even shrimps, crabs and various echinoderms such as sea urchins and star fish are sometimes eaten by tope.

Although by world standards tope are not what might be called 'big fish,' they are one of the largest caught in British waters. At the time of writing the British rod-caught record stands at 74 lb 11 oz, a weight which is only exceeded by 12 other entries, about half of which are similar fish such as porbeagle, mako and blue shark.

Like the blue shark and several other species in its class, tope are viviparous, giving birth to possibly as many as 50, but more usually around 30, perfectly formed live young. The females frequently come into quite shallow areas in summer for the young to be born.

Tope are widespread. During recent years quite a lot has been learned about their distribution and habits, facts which have surprised many. However, before looking more closely at the knowledge we have gleaned as a result of the work done by several groups of very dedicated anglers, as well as by various official agencies, it is worth noting some of the places where tope are caught.

From Donegal Bay in the North West of Ireland, around the north coast to Strangford and Carlingford Loughs, in fact along the east coast, there are few areas which do not offer the chance of catching tope of 40, 50 or even 60 lb.

Indeed, Strangford Lough has yielded tope to $60\frac{3}{4}$ lb, and during 1979, a tope weighing $66\frac{1}{2}$ lb was caught in Carlingford Lough.

On the west coast, for example in Tralee Bay, there are, at times, large packs of tope which provide excellent sport.

Greystones, near Wicklow in the south east, is yet another area where tope are caught.

From the south west coast of Scotland to Wales and then north Cornwall there are a number of excellent tope fishing grounds. Similar remarks can be made regarding parts of the south coast, off Hampshire and Sussex in particular.

The Thames estuary, and also the Wash, are areas where tope have been caught regularly over the years.

I say 'have been caught' because tope, in common with so many other species, do not seem to be as plentiful now as they were ten or more years ago; but that is another story.

One might reasonably ask if these fish are to a large extent 'residential', or do they display a regular and readily discernible migratory tendency.

For example, mackerel and whiting are well known for their seasonal movements, as indeed are many other species, but until the late 1970s, not a lot was known about the migratory habits of tope.

The Fisheries Laboratory at Lowestoft, a Ministry of Agriculture, Fisheries and Food establishment, is constantly involved in the study of fish and their seasonal movement, principally, I imagine, with commercial interests in mind.

During 1959 whilst research vessels were catching, tagging and then releasing various species of cartilaginous fish such as skate, ray and dogfish, they also, but quite incidentally, tagged a number of tope that were caught during normal fishing operations.

From 1959 until 1963 no less than 75 tope were fitted with Petersen discs (special tags which were attached to the leading dorsal fin), all these fish being taken in trawls.

During the period from the end of May until July, 1966, a further 55 tope were rod-

Tope fishing – and judging by the line a tope has been hooked

caught, tagged and then released by anglers fishing off Rhyl, North Wales.

In 1970, the Selsey Tope Fishers Specimen Club was formed, and from then, until 1976, no less than 361 tope were caught, tagged and released by group members.

As the 1960s were ending, and as a result of complaints from anglers regarding falling catches, the Irish organisation, Inland Fisheries Trust, also began an investigation into the mystery which surrounded tope migration.

Now, two reports have been published, one entitled "The Migrations of Tope, Galeorhinus galeus (L) in the Eastern North Atlantic as determined by Tagging," and "Tope, Galeorhinus galeus (L) Migrations from Irish coastal waters, and notes on Irish specimens."

The former has two authors, M.J. Holden of the Fisheries Laboratory, Lowestoft, and R.G. Horrod, secretary of Selsey Tope Fishers Specimen Club; the

Irish report is the work of Dr. P. Fitzmaurice.

It is interesting to note that as a result of various experiences, the Irish experiment was conducted with Roto tags from the start, whereas the Fisheries Laboratory, the North Wales anglers and also the Selsey group used Petersen discs.

For several reasons, not least of which would seem to be the fact that Rototags carry more information, and so are more likely to be recognised for what they are and thus returned, the use of Petersen discs

conclusion reached by both reports.

Consider some of the details provided by the Holden/Horrod paper.

A male fish tagged off the north coast of Ireland on 22 May 1963 was recaptured 88 days later in the vicinity of Blackpool.

Another male tope, this time caught off the North Wales coast, was tagged and released on 3 June 1966, but 3962 days were to pass before this particular fish was recaptured. On 8 April 1977 it was caught off the south-west corner of Ireland.

However, it is the Selsey group's tagging

The beautiful slim-line tope provides good sport in British waters

has been discontinued.

However, that is a side issue, albeit an interesting one which also takes into consideration such things as the possibility of tags being bitten off, and fouling nets and so tearing free.

The Holden/Horrod report, whilst not coming to any firm conclusions, certainly presents evidence supporting the theory that tope do undertake long migratory journeys, possibly for reproduction.

There is a definite southerly pattern to the migratory movement of many fish, but then some, admittedly a minority, appear to act in a contrary matter. This is a

programme which gives the bulk of the evidence provided by the returns. This must be so, because of the large number of fish they have caught, tagged and released from one easily identifiable area.

Apart from a few interesting exceptions, the tope released off Selsey have followed a path which leads from off the West Sussex coast, down to the North West coast of Africa and the Canaries.

It is a route which can be traced by noting the places of recapture. The dates on which the fish were caught for a second time do not, for very obvious reasons, give any indication regarding the wandering or even the possible ultimate destination of individual fish. It could well be that a fish finally caught off Gran Canaria had in fact followed the line indicated by the recapture points of other fish. On the other hand it may have travelled in an almost direct line.

However, the report by Dr Fitzmaurice says "Wheeler (1969) states that tope are found over gravel and sand bottoms up to a depth of 30 fathoms, and that they are rather solitary shallow water species, but occasionally they occur in small shoals."

miles south of the Isle of Wight, and then 12 miles south.

We then find that Alderney, the most northerly of the Channel Islands is mentioned, as are the Needles at the western end of the Isle of Wight, and also Carteret which is on the Cherbourg Peninsula and south of Alderney, all in the general west and southerly path from Selsey Bill.

Next in line is Pointe-de-Penmach, and then south again to the Bay of Archachon. At this juncture it is interesting to note that a fish recaptured off the Pointe-de-

Accepting this statement as a general guide, then possibly all the tope migrating towards the north west coast of Africa and the Canary Islands, do follow, as far as possible, the coastal path indicated by the recapture points of various tagged fish.

Ignoring the number of days each of the following fish had been at liberty after being tagged, one can see a very definite route beginning to emerge as one looks at the recapture points on a map.

Starting at Selsey, the route goes west to the Nab Tower which lies between Selsey Bill and the south east tip of the Isle of Wight. The next place of recapture is 10

Penmach had been at liberty for 191 days, another at Gironde for 282 days, and one recaptured in the Bay of Archachon 714 days.

It is possible that all these fish were part of a general and continuous migratory movement, and it just happened that they were recaptured at different times and places along a route they travelled quite regularly?

Following the coastline from the Bay of Archachon, and continuing along the northern coast of Spain, we come to Punta Galea, Bilbao, where a tope was recaptured that had been free for 164 days.

Tope fishing is popular off Ireland. This fisherman has hooked one in Tralee Bay

Another taken off the Portuguese coast had been at liberty for 108 days. Cadiz Bay saw the recapture of a tope 1317 days after its original capture and tagging.

Returning for a moment to northern Spain, Bilbao, one fish taken there had been at liberty for only 90 days, quite a contrast to the other taken in the same general area which was recaptured after 164 days.

Morocco, north west Africa, and still on a southerly path, saw the taking of yet another tope which had been tagged off Selsey, and this fish had been free for 691 days.

A similar period, 730 days, had passed between the tagging and recapture of yet another tope which was caught off Cassablanca.

At the time of writing, Gran Canaria is the most southerly point from which a tag has been returned. A fish originally tagged on 29 May 1978 was recaptured there 459 days later on 31 August 1979.

Is it not fascinating that another tope that was marked on 25 May 1974 should also be recaptured off Gran Canaria, 1206 days later, during September 1977?

Having established one possible migratory route, there is yet another line which some seem to follow. It is not particularly distinct, nor have many fish been recaptured along its path, but for some reason a few tope turn eastwards from Selsey, and then head up Channel towards the Straits of Dover.

For example, on 8 July 1977 a tope was tagged off Selsey, and 701 days later it was recaptured off Bognor Regis some 10 miles or so east of the 'Bill'. Yet another was recaptured south east of Hastings after 283 days, whilst a fish tagged in May 1976 was caught again, 140 days later eight miles north of Folkestone.

In this general direction there is also Boulogne, where a tope was caught after 143 days at liberty. Helgoland Island, off the coast of Denmark saw the recapture of a tope that had been free for 790 days, from July 1976 until September 1978, and as if to prove how quickly these fish can move around, just 87 days after being tagged off Selsey, a tope was recaptured off Trimingham, Norfolk.

Travelling directly, that fish must have been covering about 3 miles or so each day. In fact, it probably did a lot more, especially when tidal factors are taken into consideration.

Apart from one or two 'rogues' such as, for example, the fish which was recaptured, and then again returned to the sea alive off Padstow, north Cornwall, those tope tagged off Selsey seem to have conformed to a pattern which appears to run from the North Sea to the Canary Islands.

There is, of course, no scientific proof that this is a definite migratory route, for as the authors of the Holden/Horrod paper point out: "The recapture of four tope close to

Below A tope being tagged before its return to the water

Bottom A collection of fine tope, the largest being 44 lb

their release positions after an interval of a multiple of almost exactly one year, suggests a movement with an annual basis although, alternatively, such returns could depend upon seasonal fishing activity on fish which were present throughout the year."

In his report, Dr Fitzmaurice also notes the southerly migration. He says: "On examination of the recapture details, it can be seen that from the long distance recaptures (referring to the Inland Fisheries Trust research programme) there is a distinct pattern of southerly migration. However, some of the recaptures in Irish waters show a northerly migration pattern.

"A clear-cut picture does not emerge from the migration patterns of the Irish tope. This may also be said of tope tagged off the British coasts."

Dr Fitzmaurice goes on to make a comment which is similar to that made in the Holden/Horrod report:

"Some Irish tope have been recaptured close to the point of release and up to two years after tagging. One of these fish was recaptured only four miles from the point of release after 405 days at liberty. It was re-released and caught 405 days later only 52 miles from the original place of tagging. This could mean that the fish stayed in Irish waters during the whole of that period or it could have migrated south and back again twice during that period. Alternatively tope when they reach a certain stage in their life history could migrate southwards and not return to our waters."

The overall picture created by the two reports is not only fascinating, showing as it does the great distances which these ocean nomads can wander, but it also brings home the importance of international co-operation in such ventures. As Dr Fitzmaurice comments: "It would appear that the only solution to these suggestions (previous paragraph referring to fish staying in Irish waters etc) would be a tagging operation similar to our own in areas such as the Spanish coasts (Atlantic and Mediterranean) the Gran Canaria Islands and the Azores Islands."

That tope are an important angling species cannot be denied, nor can the fact that their numbers seem to be declining. Add to these facts the important points relating to their slow growth, and conservation becomes even more important.

Tope are considered to be both relatively long lived and slow growing, and scientific evidence points out that a female is not mature until 10 years old. Therefore, is it not time that more of these fish were released after capture, instead of landing them merely to claim a trophy or have a picture taken? Have we not reached the point at which certificates for the release of such fish are preferable to cups or shields for killing them?

"But," some might ask, "are they not large and powerful creatures with fearsome teeth-lined jaws? Is it reasonable to suggest that one should risk injury merely to release such a fish?"

If a tope is caught by accident rather than design then possibly such an argument is valid – but not, in my opinion, if one deliberately sets out to fish for them. I have satisfied myself on many occasions that killing a tope is seldom justified, for

A 28-lb tope being weighed on board before being returned to the sea

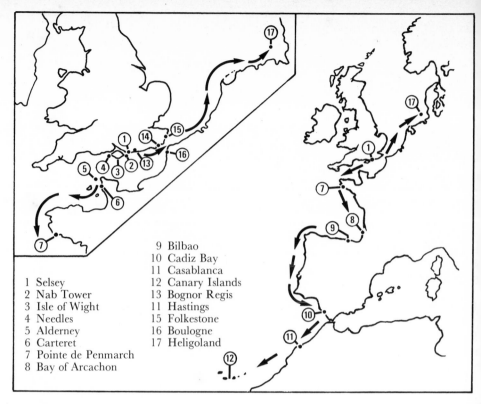

1 Selsey
2 Nab Tower
3 Isle of Wight
4 Needles
5 Alderney
6 Carteret
7 Pointe de Penmarch
8 Bay of Arcachon
9 Bilbao
10 Cadiz Bay
11 Casablanca
12 Canary Islands
13 Bognor Regis
11 Hastings
15 Folkestone
16 Boulogne
17 Heligoland

unhooking them is usually a relatively straightforward thing, and taking them from the water is uncomplicated, if both care and discipline are exercised.

Tope angling must be considered a specialised sport; but not so much from the tackle standpoint as from the techniques associated with finding, hooking, landing and then releasing them.

As for tackle, I would not look for anything more than a 20-lb class rod, except when fishing an area where tidal conditions make using heavier equipment absolutely essential.

A nylon covered steel trace is needed, as not only are their teeth capable of cutting through nylon or a braided line, but a tope can and sometimes will roll around and chafe the line with its extremely rough skin.

Never use less than six feet of trace, and always have a quick release fitment between trace and line to facilitate handling as soon as the fish is boated.

All the well-documented tope angling techniques stand the test of time, and apart from one or two local tricks which are employed to overcome specific problems which relate to particular areas, there is not much to add except comments regarding bait, the importance of distance between

hook and weight, and the actual amount of lead used.

In my opinion the most effective tope bait is freshly caught mackerel, but as these fish are steadily becoming a scarce commodity, it could be that before long the ethics of using one as bait might be questioned!

Others, and there are quite a few, use flat fish such as flounder and sand dabs, and there are those who favour a fillet of bream as tope bait.

As far as I am concerned these are no longer bait fish, but in any case I would prefer to use cuttle or squid even if the flat fish and bream were freely available.

The distance between hook and weight should, in my opinion, be not less than about say 12 to 15-ft and even up to about 30 ft is not overlong on some occasions.

This extra distance (over and above the length of the nylon covered steel trace) is gained by fixing a stop on the main line, so that the boom carrying the lead rests against it. A matchstick can be used as a stop, but when wet some will bend instead of snapping cleanly and falling clear when reeled in against the rod's top ring. A short length of strong nylon, or even a piece of the plastic casing used to cover "bell wire" is adequate; these items will come through he rings without causing damage, or they an be pulled out easily allowing the knot to collapse.

Never use more lead than is needed to keep the bait where you want it to be. As the force exerted by the tidal flow either increases or slackens, so the amount of lead must also change to match.

Despite their size and power, I have always found tope to be very suspicious of the restriction they must feel if they lift and run with a bait held down by a heavy lead; and this is despite the fact that, in theory, the line should run freely through the boom's eye.

It is therefore also important that the reel be set in such a way that line, and plenty of it, is instantly and freely available as the fish makes its first run.

The tricks which a hooked tope might play are legion. Whilst fishing in relatively shallow water I have known them to leap like a salmon; run up-tide hard and fast, and then totally change direction and head for the boat with all the speed of a torpedo. They will run under the craft from which you are fishing, and whilst you are adjusting to this manoeuvre, they might well double back and then take off again in yet another direction.

There is no doubting the tope's ability to test your angling skill, but the best, and in my opinion the most satisfying part of this sport, is when the fish is finally unhooked and released back into its element.

Performing this seemingly difficult task calls for both discipline and complete understanding between the two anglers involved, and make no mistake, for safety there should be two.

Here I make suggestions relating to the procedure which can be followed in a small boat, say 16 feet or so – on a larger craft the sequence can be modified or adjusted to fit the changed circumstances.

As soon as the fish is beaten and is being brought alongside, the angler must sit, possibly amid-ships, and allow his companion in the stern to give final directions.

For stability, place yourselves on opposite sides; the fish handler should kneel, and as the fish is brought into position

Tope can rarely be caught from the shore, but one place where it is possible is Trevose Head, near Padstow, north Cornwall

grasp it by the leading dorsal fin and around the wrist (the narrow section just forward of the tail fin), and in one quick movement lift it over the side. I would recommend wearing a pair of leather palmed gardening gloves. These will give adequate protection throughout the whole operation.

As the fish comes over the side the angler should place his rod in a safe position, and immediately unhook the trace at the link.

The handler pins the fish's tail with one foot (preferably wearing a rubber boating shoe!) and holds the jaws wide, the leather palms protecting both hands from the teeth. The angler can then remove the hook with a pair of pliers.

It sounds difficult, but apart from my own experiences, the Selsey group have dealt with hundreds of tope in this way.

Many would argue, and I am certainly one of them, that if you are not prepared to deal with a tope in this or a similar manner then maybe when general conservation measures are taken into consideration, tope fishing is not for you.